5 —
WBS

American Art
Collector

ALCOVE BOOKS
Berkeley, California

D1010015

American Art
Collector

Editor:
Tom Palmer

Assistant Editors:
Aileen Kim, Chingchi Yu

Jurors:
Howard Eige, Jan Christensen Heller

July 2007 • Volume 3, Book 4

American Art Collector is published quarterly in January, April, July, and October by Alcove Books, 930 Dwight Way #7, Berkeley, CA 94710.

ANNUAL SUBSCRIPTIONS are $29. Periodicals postage pending at Berkeley, California. ISSN# 1556-6781.

POSTMASTER: send address changes to New Address, Alcove Books, 930 Dwight Way #7, Berkeley, CA 94710.

BACK ISSUES contact Chingchi Yu, Alcove Books, 930 Dwight Way #7, Berkeley, CA 94710 or 510.644.3534.

Information is from sources deemed reliable. The publisher assumes no liability for loss caused by errors, omissions, or any other cause. Copyright © 2007. All rights reserved. Printed in Hong Kong.

Front cover:
SHOT UP OLD RUSTY CAR. Lyn Smith

Back cover:
WARTHOG PITCHER. Carol Wedemeyer

Right, top:
CARIBBEAN SWIMMER. Debra Maddox

Right, bottom:
FAIRIE CIRCLE 6. Mark Chatterley

American Art Collector presents a juried collection of original art and fine craft from across the United States. The work shown here is all hand-made and one-of-a-kind or part of a limited series.

The artists' works can be seen at galleries and shows listed in the Venue directory. Many artists also accept direct commissions from buyers.

The venues listed are merely a sample and subject to change. When possible, refer to the artist's website for a current show schedule and gallery list.

Tom Palmer

Editor

CONTENTS

Orhan Alpaslan

Edgewater, MD
www.orhanalpaslan.com

ARTIST IN HIS STUDIO. Oil on canvas. 20" x 16"

"My art is narrative impressionism. I try to reveal my feelings. The long creation journey of the artist is depicted in this painting, which is a lonely, uneasy, and thoughtful process. At the background depths and mirror are expression of the artist's inner world." Venue: MFA Circle Gallery.

Lisa Ambler

Denver, CO • 303.321.0058
artglee@aol.com

PLAYING WITH SNOW - 3. Oil on canvas. 30" x 24"

"Currently, painting 'distracted realism' works, I am having great fun creating images that are neither entirely realistic nor completely abstract. It is an amazing adventure to explore the complex shapes and colors of creation."

UNTITLED. Reversed painted acrylic on acrylic. 24" x 12"

"I seek to create work that transcends time and culture, paintings that speak on fundamental terms, and ultimately to everyone. Utilizing a reductive aesthetic with fields of vibrant color, the work functions on a base or primal level. The colors are at play, often jostling for your attention."

Maude Andrade

Albuquerque, NM • 505.379.0208
www.maude-andrade.com

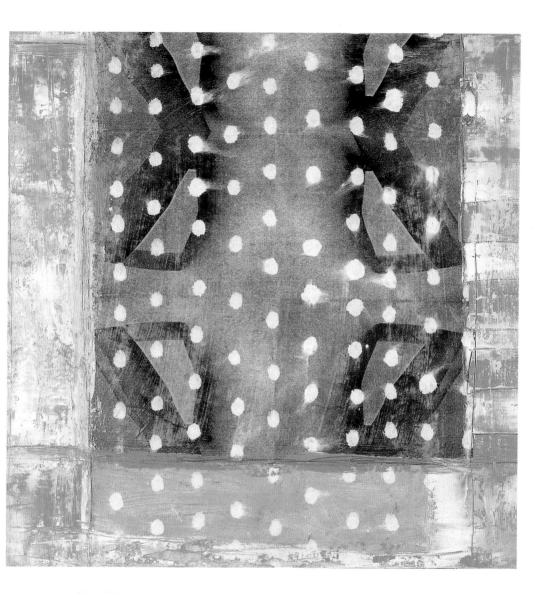

SANDSTONE MIRROR. Acrylic, collage, ink, and oil on board. 24" x 24" x 3"

"Dichotomies fascinate me, such as simple/complex, ancient/modern, order/chaos. These themes influence my collages of distorted photos and art papers. Working in mixed media is similar to speaking different languages, allowing me to paint a story with different voices." Venues: Mariposa Gallery, Bowman/Bloom, Shy Rabbit Contemporary Arts.

Emalee Andre

Palm Beach Gardens, FL • 561.625.0134
www.emaleeart.com

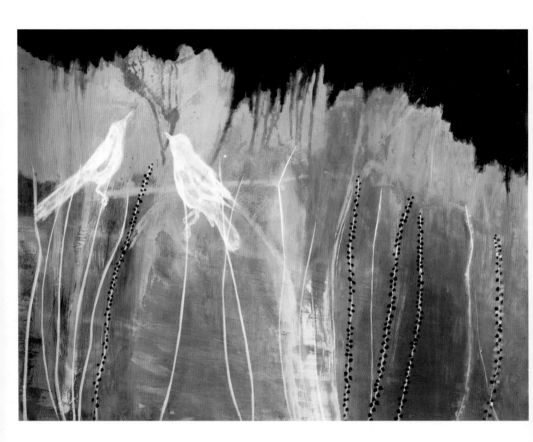

BIRD SPACE SERIES #4. Mixed media on watercolor paper. 22" x 30"

"Experimental and abstract painting allows me to infuse the work with my imagination using a variety of materials. I am motivated by the challenge of interpreting an idea, a figure, or an image in a manner that allows multiple interpretations by the viewer." Venues: Creation Art Gallery & Studios Gallery, Gallery St. Thomas.

Monica Araoz

Austin, TX • 512.415.8267
www.maraozgallery.com

EARTH ELEMENTS. Acrylic on canvas. 72" x 48"

"The basic beauty of Mother Earth inspires me to paint. I see wonder in the variation of color
tones in a mere pebble, in the rough texture of a tree trunk, or in the cracked pattern formed by
sun-baked soil. Then I try to make obvious the greatness of the simple." Venues: Art on 5th. Gallery,
Stephanie Ward Gallery, Art + Artisans Consulting.

Bob Armstrong

San Francisco, CA • 415.515.8815
www.bobarmstrongart.com

HONEYCOMB AND QUINCE II. Acrylic on canvas. 40" x 30"

"I paint the beauty in the textural richness of the natural world around me: the movement of water down a fountain, the arabesque of a leaf as it floats in water, and the unexpected geometry of a honeycomb. My paintings use careful color harmonies, physical texture, and metaphor to celebrate these visual wonders." Venue: Artists Guild of San Francisco.

MY PIECE OF THE SKY. Oil on canvas. 48" x 48"

"This work has arisen from my explorations in ascertaining significance. The idea of random acts coalescing into the creation of meaning entices me in my recent series *Random Acts*. The resulting color field abstraction is the transporter connecting these spontaneous, seemingly random marks with definition contained in the title." Venues: SFMOMA Artists Gallery, Casey and Associates, Art4Business.

Jocelyn Audette

Calistoga, CA • 707.942.5380
www.jocelynaudette.com

AFTER THE STORM, LAGUNA DE SANTA ROSA. Encaustic on panel. 24" x 24"

"The joy of discovering new places and a desire to intimately understand and connect with the landscapes that inspire me is a lifelong passion. My work explores the diversity and drama of the land, its geology, and the sculptural effects of light, water, and weather. This piece captures the Laguna de Santa Rosa during the rainy season; in the spring and summer the area is grassland."
Venues: Quicksilver Mine Company, Exploding Head Gallery, Elder Art Gallery.

Kate Solari Baker

Sausalito, CA • 415.331.0750
katesbaker@comcast.net

GOOD FRIENDS II. Oil on canvas. 48" x 36"

"My recent paintings tend to be figures in a very shallow picture plane. I prefer to work on canvas that has been prepped with a total color ground, so the color influences every part of the painting."

Pat Banks

Richmond, KY • 859.527.3334
patbanks@dishmail.net

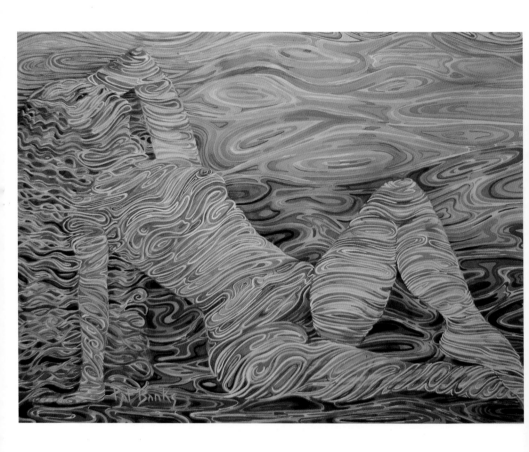

WATER GIRL. Watercolor. 22" x 30"

"The idea for *Water Girl* evolved over a period of four years. To me she became a symbol of our origins, our evolution, and our ultimate responsibility for our water. The visual texture of light and water as an elemental was a challenge to envision and a key to the success the piece." Venues: The Artisan Center, Kaviar Forge Gallery, Gallery on Main.

Judith Barath

Oak Brook, IL • 630.850.9441
www.judithbarathart.com

FALL IN THE ARBORETUM. Oil on canvas. 24" x 36"

"I paint my surroundings, my flowers, and the landscape around my Oak Brook home. I look for harmony and simple beauty—expressing the essence of a subject through detail, color arrangement, and composition."

K. B. Basseches

Richmond, VA • 804.254.1769
kbb@kbbasseches.com

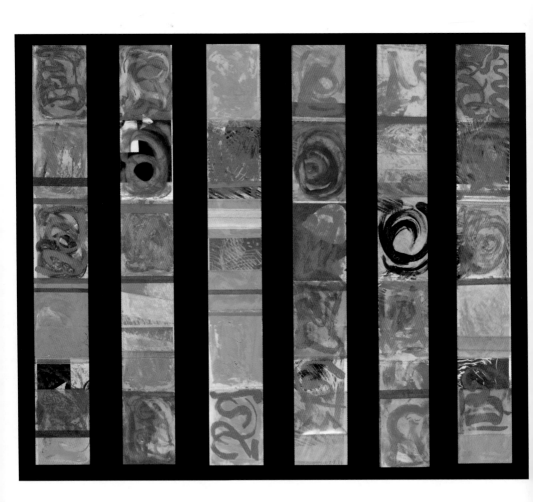

UNTITLED #1-6, OF BLOOD AND WATER SERIES. Sewn and painted photographic collages. 83" h

"My artwork expresses personal reactions to universal themes. As a new member of one of the biggest clubs, I realized that for its apparent visibility, parenting is ultimately a private act. Through abstracted symbols and riotous colorations, this series makes public the exhilarating experience of being a first-time parent." Venue: Center City Arts.

Judy Staples Becker

Rohnert Park, CA • 707.664.1839
heyjude@vbbn.com

ALAMERE FALLS, PT. REYES. Pastel on La Carte sanded paper. 31" x 22"

"I've been captivated by the coastline ever since moving to California. Happening upon this scene on the Point Reyes shoreline, one crisp, fall day, I knew I had to paint it. The sun glistening on the falling water, the dramatic shadows of the rocks, the vivid colors of the ice-plant all made me happy to be alive!" Venues: Northbay Artworks, Marin Open Studios.

Deborah Bertola

Sausalito, CA • 415.279.5103
www.dbertola.com

PRESERVED LEMONS. Oil on linen. 16" x 20"

"I am primarily known as a *plein air* landscape painter and for animal portraits. Last year, I was injured, and consequently confined to my studio, where I discovered abstract painting. In the past, my work has been described as highly individual and sensitive, with particular focus on color. This new direction has encouraged my interest in color to evolve, unfettered by realism. These are joyous paintings." Venues: SFMOMA Artists Gallery, The River Gallery, Bolinas Museum.

Jose Betancourt

Winchester, TN • 931.968.1013
www.josebetancourt.com

WIGWAM III. Gelatin silver print. 20" x 24"

"My fictional panoramic landscapes come together inside the camera as continuous uncut frames on the film strip. These vertical frames are each a single moment followed by continuous moments as I scan the scene from left to right. The scenes are usually three to seven frames."
Venues: Willis Gray Gallery, Sewanee University Art Gallery, Motlow Art Gallery.

Carole Dodson Bigot

San Rafael, CA
www.carolebigot.com

GARLIC. Oil on canvas. 18" x 36"

"As in life, nothing has dimension without both a light and a dark side. I love to explore and exaggerate those juxtapositions. The colors and intensities I choose create a drama and liveliness in my paintings that is a true representation of my passion for realism." Venues: Marin Open Studios, Studio Gallery San Francisco, The Art League of Northern California Gallery.

Nan Standish Blake

Austin, TX
nanblake@texas.net

PLACE FOR A TEA PARTY. Giclée print. 12.5" x 19"

"A gathering in the air and light of Paris that is fraught with disconnection. The actors have played their parts, and heads avoid the glare of critic and colleague alike."

Patricia Blau

San Rafael, CA • 415.258.9325
www.pblau.com

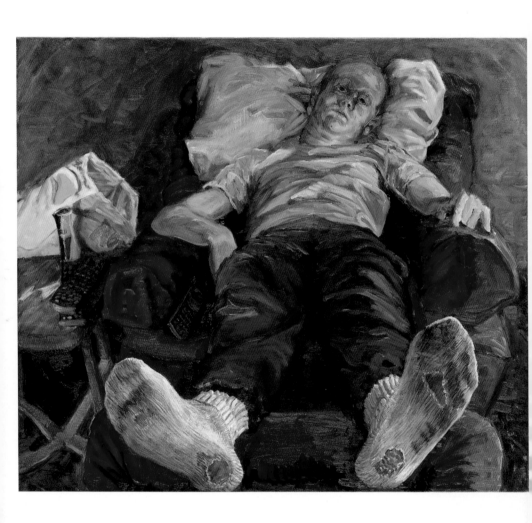

IN THE ZONE. Oil on linen. 26" x 30"

"In The Zone is another work in my series on life in America." Venue: Glass Garage Gallery.

Richard Bolingbroke

San Francisco, CA • 415.863.5654
www.rbolingbroke.com

FULL CIRCLE. Watercolor on paper. 40" x 40"

"My recent paintings from the series *Rituals and Meditations* are shrines to the magic and mystery of life. They open windows onto the paradoxical dualities of existence and bear witness to the never-ending gift that is this world." Venue: Mowen Solinski, South Dakota Art Museum, Charles Allis Museum.

Jane Booth

Spring Hill, KS • 913.592.2688
www.janebooth.com

SHE FOUND THE LAST DUCKLING AND TUCKED IT UNDER HER WING. Acrylic on canvas. 13" x 13"

"I paint to express how the world touches the senses—how moments sound, how hot or cold they are, their softness or roughness, the chaos or peace that is generated. In life, these moments evaporate as they appear. It is a joy to set them on a canvas to consider."

Dana Boussard

Arlee, MT • 406.726.3357
www.danaboussard.com

HUNTING IN MONTANA. Mixed media. 19" x 15"

"In my Montana studio I overlook the majestic Rocky Mountains and rolling valley grasslands. All of it is inhabited by wildlife that succumbs to the hunter's gun every fall. In this artwork, I've taken our country's fascination with firearms to the next level…camouflaged hunters and vulnerable prey. It's not just for wildlife anymore."

Orestes Bouzon

Miami, FL • 305.233.6989
www.bouzonart.com

ARTESANA Y LA ORQUIDIA. Oil on canvas. 30" x 24"

"I use the movements of the sea as my fluid inspiration. By means of curvaceous lines and vivid colors, I express the beauty of the feminine figure. My style has a romantic/mystical feeling, which is totally figurative and open to the imagination."

Erin Brooks

Pittsford, NY
erincbrooks@gmail.com

ANGEL. Watercolor and ink. 18" x 30"

"Good morning springtime! Now is the time to drink good wine and fish! Cast your 'Angel' into the river and chase away the gloom of the winter. This painting brought me out of the gloomy gray winter and into the bright colors of spring...inspired by the loving husband who brought me the flowers." Venue: High Falls Gallery.

Sharon Bond Brown

Denver, CO • 303.297.9831
www.patternshopstudio.com

ST. LOUIS SPRING. Oil on masonite. 36" x 30"

"I'm fascinated by what home photographers inadvertently catch—images that are casual and non-reverential, the subjects captured without their masks on, the scene not lit or staged. I try to capture slices of time, evocative moments in ordinary lives." Venues: Pattern Shop Studio, Weilworks, Foothills Art Center.

Mary Bruns

Cave Creek, AZ • 480.862.9757
www.marybrunsart.com

A LIGHT EXISTS IN SPRING. Oil on canvas. 48" x 60"

"I paint realism because I love the light, the colors, the arrangements of how things appear
next to one another; the richness of the paint locks time into place from mind to canvas.
Ordinary things become most extraordinary when we take the time to look at them."
Venue: The Museum of Contemporary Art of Georgia Permanent Collection.

Rulei Bu

Boyds, MD • 301.916.5991
www.burulei.com

NEW YORK SUNSET. Oil on canvas. 18" x 24"

"I am interested in the structure of buildings and boats, and the reflections and colors of water also fascinate me. I enhance the colors and textures of my harbor scenes to suggest the effects of light, making my painting both dramatic and vivid." Venues: Framer's Choice Gallery, Prince Royal Gallery, Alvear Studio.

Mary Burke

Berrien Springs, MI • 269.471.1724
www.maryburkeart.com

SEED BED. Acrylic and pencil on canvas. 30" x 24"

"I enjoy combining a variety of random marks with those that are placed with care. Some are non-figurative, while others reference reality. For me, a minimal, child-like scribble on a raw surface is an exciting reminder of a primitive past." Venues: Coady Contemporary, Hudson Gallery, Sunday Afternoon Gallery.

Carol Ann Cain

Niceville, FL • 850.729.1709
www.carolanncain.com

BOGGY ANGLE. Acrylic on canvas. 48" x 36"

"Over the years, I have formed a bond with the bogs in my area. They have become like
a mute friend who has granted me permission to translate her for others to hear. She
ponders, she gestures wildly…I simply seek to turn my canvas to the angle of her pantomime."
Venues: Beverly McNeil Gallery, Matt Jones Gallery, Soho Myriad.

Judy Campbell

Denver, CO • 720.352.4848
www.judycampbellart.com

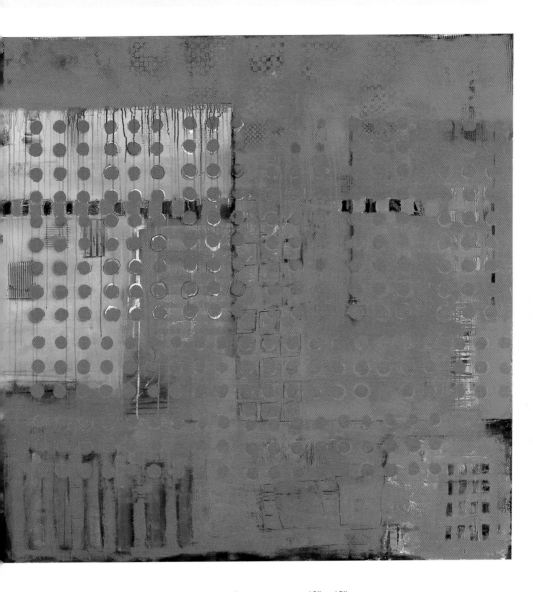

ON FIRE. Acrylic on canvas. 60" x 60"

"The past few years I painted with very subtle colors. I had previously painted only with intensely bright colors so I wanted a change. But, for this piece, I decided to try bright colors again. I added texture and shapes but maintained the intensity and I'm please with the result."
Venues: Water Street Gallery, Lydon Fine Art, Artizen Fine Arts.

Patricia A. Canney

Minneapolis, MN • 612.387.6225
www.pacanney.com

SPECIAL OCCASION. Oil on canvas. 24" x 24"

"These new store fronts, dressmaker, and costume paintings are figurative without the figure. I have often found subjects in coffee shops and restaurants where people may be working or lost in thought. Store fronts and back alleys, beaches, and back yards, the main street or the empty room. I am drawn to that certain kind of light that catches an unguarded moment." Venues: J. Pierce White Oak Gallery, Abend Gallery Fine Art, Huff Harrington Fine Art.

Katie Caprara

Shawnee-on-Delaware, PA • 201.874.7173
katie_whitesell@yahoo.com

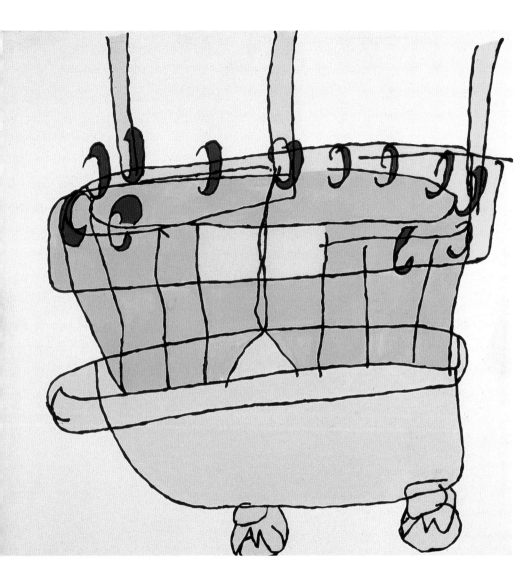

CLAWFOOT TUB. Acrylic on canvas. 18" x 18"

"I have great memories. I draw on my love of my past to find my subjects for my paintings. I consider each painting a vintage still life, expressed with colors that are retro-reminiscent. I use color to conjure nostalgia, and objects that shepherd in yesterday."

YELLOW JOY. Oil on canvas. 3' x 4'

"My intention is to see deeper than the physical qualities within a landscape. I choose locations that have a certain wildness, where the essence and story are more than contours and lines. My passion is to capture the light that illuminates our landscape with my paintbrush. As a California Colorist, I find inspiration for oil paintings near my studio in Sausalito, the vineyards of wine country, and in Tuscany." Venues: William Torphy Fine Arts, Sausalito Art Festival.

WOMEN'S TOUCH. Mixed media on canvas. 72" x 48"

"My paintings combine the representational still life subject matter such as floral and fruit, with a framed window of luminous abstract imagery that uses calligraphy and collage work to reveal a more personal side. My love of music is evident as well, with the use of musical notation accentuating almost all my pieces."

Bonnie Carter

Decatur, GA • 404.290.3389
www.bonniecarter.com

STRATA. Acrylic and acrylic ink on paper. 14" x 14"

"*Strata* represents layers of earth formed in my imagination. My work is created intuitively until the painting takes on a life of its own. I use thin glazes of paint, and poured, dripped, and drizzled details to create texture." Venues: Sycamore Place Gallery, Digital Art Studio.

Perci Chester

Minneapolis, MN • 612.204.9664
www.percichester.com

SALLY DREW FORTH HER SABER. Giclée print. 36" x 45"

"Sally Drew Forth Her Saber began as a collage using varied elements, including photographic images of plant cells, glass shards, and dimensional wires. My graphic work is a reflection of my sculpture that celebrates my roots as a painter and my love of color."

Sara Clark

Richmond, VA • 804.288.2487
sclark234@yahoo.com

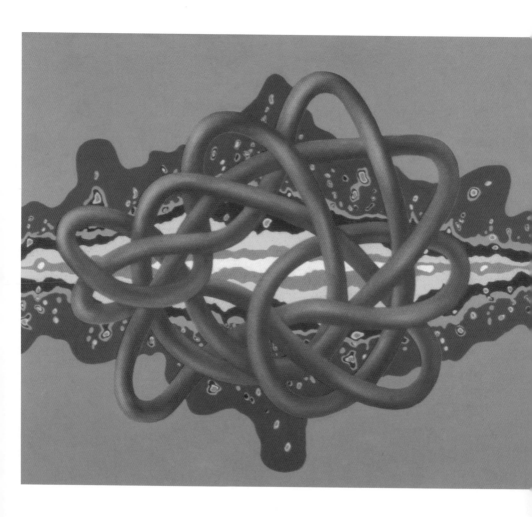

K632. Oil on canvas. 36" x 42"

"I use mathematical and scientific models as objects in an idealized world—a way of describing shape and space. For this image, I have chosen from mathematics the topological shape of a knot. In this painting, I reveal one of these knots' many possible configurations."
Venues: Ada Gallery, 1708 Gallery.

Cary Cleaver

Douglasville, GA • 770.949.5351
www.particularwomen.com

LOIRE VALLEY, FRANCE #2. Hand-colored photograph. 11" x 14"

"I start with black and white photographs, applying special oils rubbed down into the emulsion, making the images archival. Each is a unique work of art within a limited hand-printed edition. This old-fashioned technique perfectly suits my images of vanishing landscapes and cityscapes." Venues: Cultural Arts Center of Douglasville, Atlanta Celebrates Photography.

Page Coleman

Albuquerque, NM • 505.238.5071
www.pagecoleman.com

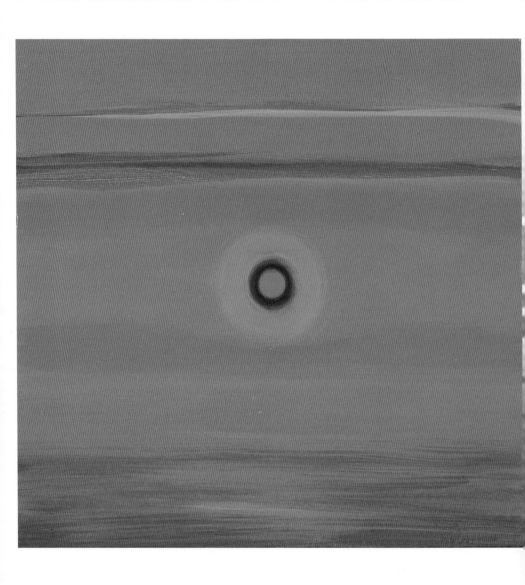

PULSE #1. Acrylic on paper. 18" x 18"

"I continue to explore ways of creating an 'other world' sense of place in my paintings. In each painting, I employ color juxtaposition and value to create a visual pulse. My paintings have always been about the land, sea, and sky. They are 'scapes reduced to their bare elements." Venues: Coleman Gallery Contemporary Art, Jay Etkin Gallery.

Joyce Agri Colvario

Boston, MA • 617.312.4241
www.joyceagricolvario.com

ANCESTORS. Photopolymer gravure print. 10" x 8"

"Recently I have become intrigued with solarplate intaglio print making. This photopolymer gravure process transfers an intriguing dimension to a digital image onto a solarplate. Printed with a manual press, the resulting permanent prints possess a rich tonal range and velvet quality characteristic of traditional photogravure."

David P. Cooke

Laguna Beach, CA • 949.933.9363
davidpcooke@aol.com

EXPECTING TO FLY. Oil on linen. 18" x 48"

"This painting is from a series of works picturing train and subway riders which are loosely autobiographical. These paintings have also been a tool to visualize the generational history of my family since arriving in America, up to present day personal and observed relationships. I create them in studio from models and imagined interiors." Venue: Winfield Gallery.

Maeve Croghan

San Francisco, CA • 415.775.6374
www.maevecroghan.com

PEDROCELLI AUTUMN. Oil on canvas. 24" x 30"

"I am particularly attracted to old and weathered forms of life. Aged trees, vines, and rocks seem to have a voice in my painting. My paintings are begun in nature and finished in the studio. At this point I work only from the memory and feeling of the original painting experience." Venues: Hunters Point Shipyard Spring and Fall Open Studios, Auberge Mendocino Gallery, William Torphy Fine Arts, SFMOMA Artists Gallery.

Sidnea D'Amico

San Francisco, CA • 415.577.8126
www.sidneadamico.com

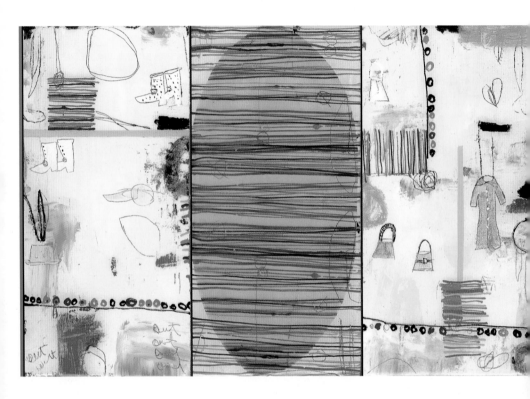

BOOTS AND HATS, DRESSES AND PURSES. Mixed media on board. 16" x 16"

"In this series I experience and explore the freedom of a child. Using organic and playful shapes I rediscover and reinvent my own observations of street graffiti and daily, common objects. Underneath the pale palette of this painting is an abstract and colorful painting which is revealed through lines I scratch and small spaces I leave uncovered."

Anne-Marie De Rivera

Tiburon, CA • 415.435.1174
originalportraits@comcast.net

A WOMAN IN BLACK. Oil on canvas. 35" x 35"

"I was attracted to the graphic nature of this painting in terms of color and shapes, and to the combination of complexity, boldness, and simplicity between the subject and the background."

GOLDEN PEONIES. Watercolor. 20" x 14"

"Painting for me is an expression of gratitude. I find it thrilling to pay homage to universality within the slow, silent dance of pattern and light. It feels celebratory to play with underlying melodic and percussive repetitions of color. While painting, I delight in undulating lines and forms, in the exquisite, unending variety of nature's palette."

Peter Dellert

Holyoke, MA • 413.534.5253
www.dellertfurniture.com

RESERVOIR MAP #6. Mixed media on board. 6" x 6"

"The new collages use leaves, paper, and old maps cut or torn and re-assembled in grids, and patterns behind an overlay of sycamore bark. This gives an overall map-like appearance, albeit one of an otherworldly nature." Venues: Chesterwood Museum, Sculpture New Hope Arts Center, Tokonoma Gallery.

Alison Denyer

Salt Lake City, UT
adenyer@earthlink.net

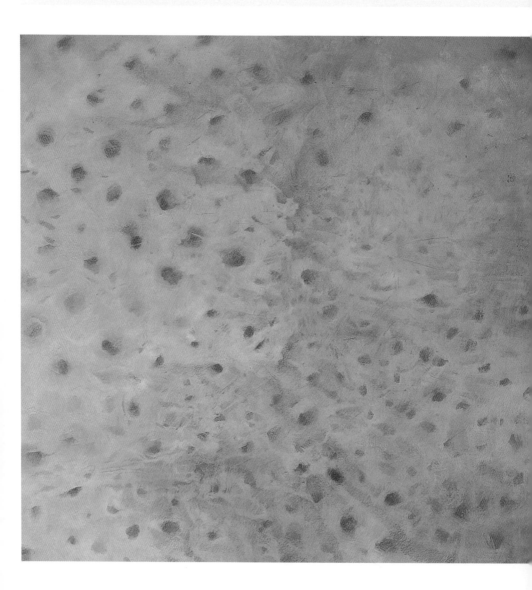

MASS. Oil, encaustic on gessoed paper. 20" x 20"

"Inspired by landscape elements, I am also fascinated by aerial views. I feel there is an interesting tension between the natural and the human-made mark on the landscape. Each work goes through a multi-layered process of paint application, and throughout this process, drawn elements are introduced."

Sam Dixon

Washington, DC • 202.545.1555
www.samdixon.org

LEMONS AND OLIVES. Oil, carbon on board. 5" x 7"

"I am primarily a watercolorist, but also work in oil and acrylics. I would like to think my art captures the essence of inspiration and temperament." Venues: Main St. Gallery, Broadway Gallery, The Weatherburn Gallery.

Monte Dolack

Missoula, MT • 406.549.3248
www.dolack.com

MONTANA POWER. Acrylic on board. 36" x 48"

"My paintings are inspired by the natural world and informed by a passionate interest in travel, art, books, and mythology. I paint luminous and dramatic encounters with nature, personalizing the images with cultural, spiritual, and social influences."

Susan Dorf

Langley, WA • 831.689.9336
www.susandorf.com

DIARY OF A LANDSCAPE. Oil on canvas. 30" x 24"

"I am interested in how a painting communicates that which is beneath the surface of how we experience our everyday lives. The essence of place holds a sense of timelessness with history and stories to tell. So does the painting process as it transforms the way we see the world." Venue: Mowen Solinsky Gallery.

Thomas Draper

New Orleans, LA • 504.523.1815
www.draperart.com

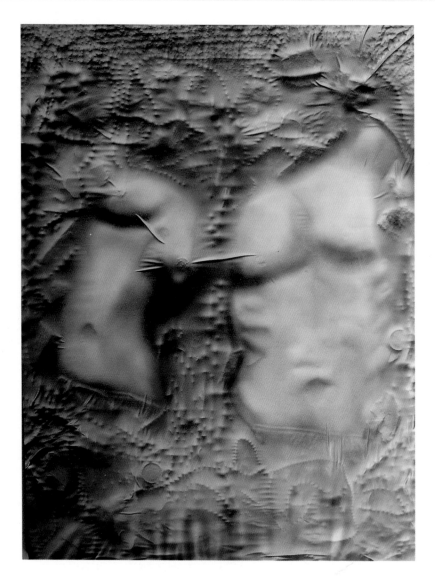

RENEW. Acrylic on canvas. 40" x 30"

"This painting uses the Mardi Gras colors of green, gold, and purple. The background of beads and doubloons was added to suggest some of the many assets New Orleans has to come back."

William Dreskin

San Anselmo, CA • 415.457.3949
www.dreskinfineart.com

DUNES AT SUNSET. Ultrachrome archival print. 20" x 30"

"I am drawn to the intricate patterns of light and shadow in these desert sand dunes. I feel inspired exploring pure abstract forms and the many strong connections between microcosm and macrocosm. You see relationships between beach sand patterns, aboriginal sacred paintings, and deep space Hubble telescope images." Venues: Marin Open Studios, Marin Society of Artists.

Paule Dubois Dupuis

San Francisco, CA • 415.987.0728
www.duboisdupuis.com

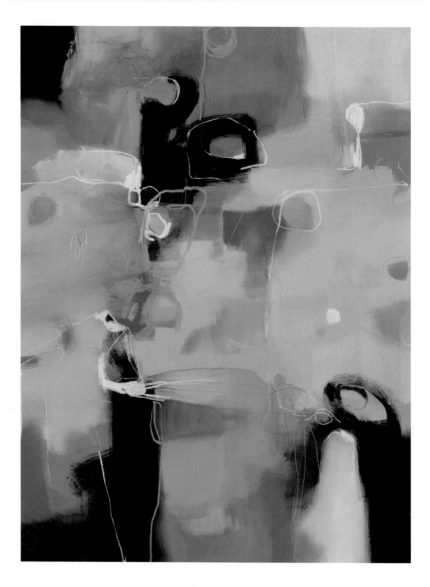

UNDERCURRENT. Oil on panel. 60" x 45"

"*Undercurrent* represent the force beneath the surface, the underlying influence that affects each individual life. The word 'undercurrent' means a tendency of feeling, opinion, or the like, in a direction contrary to what is publicly shown. The use of lines, soft greens, and blues mixed with black and white helped portray this quiet emotional quality underlying an utterance." Venues: American Art Gallery, Pamela Skinner Gallery.

Jayne Duryea

Beeville, TX • 361.358.7314
www.jayneduryea.com

EARLY MORNING LIGHT. Oil on canvas. 40" x 36"

"My objective is to create a heightened sense of color interaction—to bring a freshness or clarity to the movement of color and to explore that visual illusion that reawakens our perceptions. A major abstract element is the fluidity and movement of nature and the particular color and quality of light."

Marla E

Altamonte Springs, FL • 407.463.0762
www.marlae.com

URB ONE. Plastic, acrylic on wood. 24" x 24"

"A funny thing happened on the way to the city...In this piece, graffiti emerges from images
of buildings, as non-conventional thoughts and ideas compete for a voice in the mainstream."
Venues: Art Park, Steffanno's Fine Art, Q Gallery.

Nancy D. Eckels

Canyon Country, CA • 661.250.1068
www.nancyeckels.com

ISSUES 1. Acrylic on canvas. 24" x 24"

"Sometimes when I'm in a painting 'zone' my hand goes into auto-pilot and the subconscious takes over. The paint just seems to flow into the correct places. This was a 'zone' painting."
Venues: Lauryn Taylor Fine Art, Sarah Jessica Fine Art, La Quinta Arts Festival.

Anna W. Edwards

San Leandro, CA • 510.636.1721
www.annawedwards.com

CHITZEN ITZA. Mixed media. 48" x 36"

"This painting is from my *Yucatan* series. *Chitzen Itza* results from contemplation and reflection on the lives and culture of the Mayan people, and the ancient ruins at Chitzen Itza. I invite the viewer to look beyond the formal qualities and enjoy the surface textures and subtleties of the work."
Venues: SFMOMA Artists Gallery, Joyce Gordon Gallery, Oakland Museum of CA Collectors Gallery.

Gregory Ellison

Fairfax, CA • 415.785.8883
www.gregellison.com

THE WITNESS. Oil on canvas. 34" x 24"

"In an age where visual calories are so empty, I am drawn to art that expresses restraint, harmony, and devotion to nature. I hope that painting directly from life will help me render as we humans actually perceive." Venue: Geras-Tousignant Gallery.

Anne Embree

Santa Fe, NM • 303.570.6036
anneembree@earthlink.net

DAISY'S BEAR. Oil on board. 30" x 34"

"Through my paintings, I want the viewer to re-evaluate what we know about animals and our relationships with them as well as pushing our boundaries of what we were taught to believe each animal represented. This is done through manipulation of paint, the use of collage, and common found objects." Venues: Lanning Gallery, Jack Meier Gallery.

CRIMSON TENT. Acrylic on board. 64" x 57"

"I have long been drawn to the art of Persia, India, and the Middle East and this inspired my series of paintings entitled *Land Escapes*. These idealized landscapes invite the viewer to escape to surreal places of beauty, mystery, and intrigue."

Mary Farmer

San Rafael, CA • 415.302.4348
www.maryfarmer.com

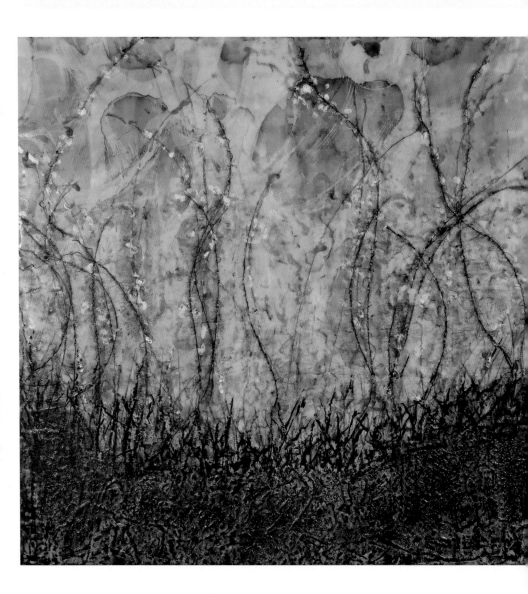

BAYOU LILIES. Mixed media on panel. 24" x 24"

"I simmer, apply, layer, and scrape an encaustic of beeswax, pigment, and resin to create painted, sculptured pieces reflecting transformation of time and graphic archaeology. Wax enriches color and offers a unique appearance of illumination from within. I explore a wide range of content, tactile possibilities, and personal revelation." Venue: ConradWilde Gallery.

Karen Folgarelli

Overland Park, KS • 913.648.6633
www.karenfolgarelli.com

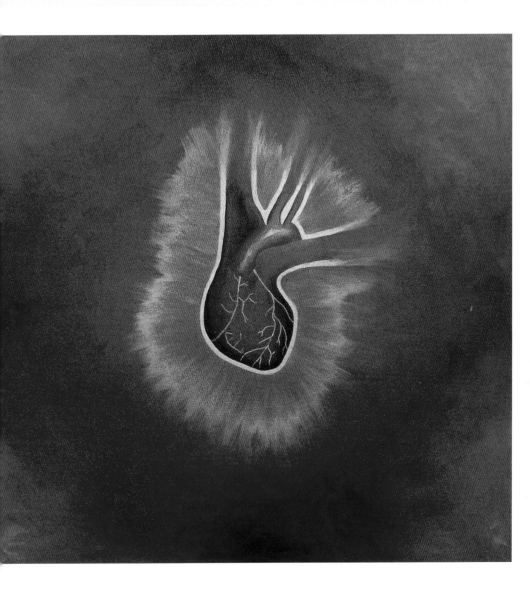

AURA HEART. Acrylic on canvas. 24" x 24"

"For me, painting embraces life in process—expressions of energy, spirit, and emotion that are feelings of the moment. By allowing this awareness to be communicated through colors, movements, and shapes, I create surpassing present boundaries with an expanded view of being, embracing life's infinite possibilities."

Louise A. Frechette

Kennebunk, ME • 207.967.2422
www.frechettegallery.com

UNSPOKEN. Soft pastel, gold leaf. 37" x 37"

"My seascape paintings are inspired by the awesome power and beauty of the Atlantic and Pacific Oceans. I paint with a wide spectrum of richly-colored soft pastels using fingers only. The pastel works often contain touches of 23k gold or silver leaf." Venues: L.A. Frechette Gallery, Christopher Bell Gallery.

Gloria Gaddis

Scottsdale, AZ • 480.951.5075
gaddis225@cox.net

COLOR FIELDS II. Oil on canvas. 36" x 36"

"There is a mystery about the painting process that pulls me in and creates a kind of magic beyond words. The *Color Field* series reflects elements of awareness, energy, and dualities that exist within the universe and on the surface of the painting." Venues: Chiaroscuro Gallery, Sue Greenwood Fine Art, Denise Roberge Gallery.

William Galarneau

San Jose, CA • 408.246.9155
www.galarneaustudios.net

BAZAAR. Acrylic on canvas. 24" x 30"

"The sun beats down on the Oriental market. A soft, warm breeze wafts the native clothing
into colorful, sinuous butterfly shapes that blend with the shimmering, heat waves."
Venues: Silicon Valley Open Studios, Quinlan Center.

Jeanne Garant

Arlington, VA • 703.486.8697
jgarant@comcast.net

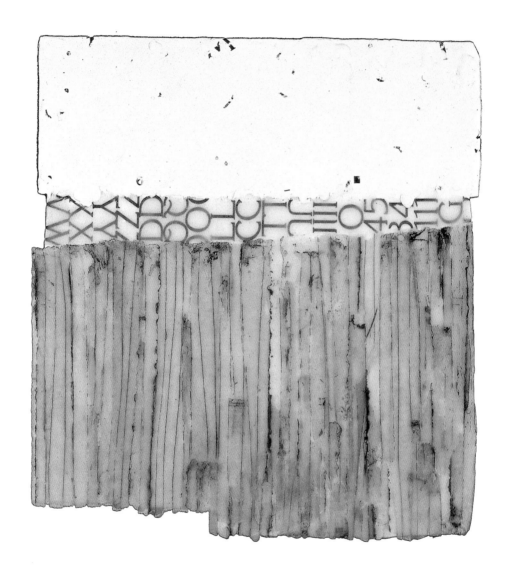

GOUDY. Encaustic on wood. 10" x 9"

"*Goudy* says it all. Stripes, text, limited color, the translucency of wax, a shaped format—some of my favorite things." Venues: Torpedo Factory Art Center, Touchstone Gallery.

KYOTO VARIATION (EUPATORIUM II). Monotype chine collé. 35" x 30"

"My work is informed by a kind of mythical nature—the power of storms, the spiritual quality of the elements, the beauty, grace, and ferocity of plants and animals—something greater than myself beyond comprehension. Painting and making monotypes is my search for the mystery within the subject, within myself." Venues: Hodges Taylor Gallery, Pelter Gallery.

Jo Ann Gentle

Pittsford, NY
www.joanngentle.com

LINWOOD REST. Whiteline print on Somerset paper. 22" x 16"

"The *Whiteline Woodblock* or *Provincetown Print* was first developed in 1915 by a group of Provincetown and Cape Cod printmakers who were devoted to the woodblock printing method. The Whiteline print is considered one of the truly American art forms besides jazz." Venues: Pat Rini Rohrer Gallery, Renaissance Gallery.

Patricia Gerkin

Alexandria, VA • 703.587.1767
www.gerkinstudios.com

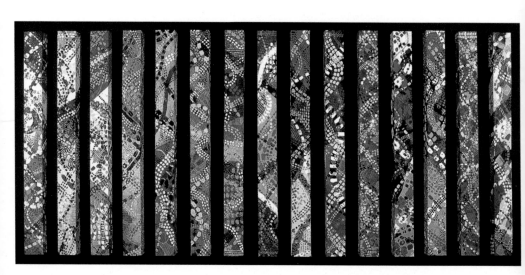

SPLENDOR IN THE GRASS #1-15. Mixed media on canvas. 48" x 4" x 4" each

"*Splendor in the Grass* explores the myriad patterns and tracks of creatures in Nature. Using images of snakes, lizards, and other reptiles as my inspiration, I develop complex compositions, retaining the natural rhythms of the Earth. The fragility of our environment, and the creatures who inhabit it, are paramount in these works." Venues: The Torpedo Factory Art Center, ArtSeen Consulting, E.C. May Art Consulting.

Ralf Gschwend

W. Palm Beach, FL • 561.655.2745
www.ralfonso.com

NATALIE, DIGITAL NUDES SERIES. Giclée print. 36" x 24"

"*Natalie* is one of twelve digitally-manipulated female nude photos from my recent *Digital Nudes, The Perception of the Female Form* series. This series digitally explores the painterly genre of pointillism, where the individual graphic elements viewed close-up look random and are not identifiable, but suddenly congeal into a recognizable form as the viewer steps away from the image. Custom personal portraits are available."

Susan Gheyssari

Chestnut Hill, MA • 617.739.1729
www.susangheyssari.com

THE GREEN PEARS. Oil on canvas. 30" x 30"

"Not to copy the object, I strive to reveal true beauty in my paintings. I do believe in strong composition of light and shadow, balance and elegant harmony between the objects in a modern manner. Peace, emotion, and joy of beauty are my inspiration to explore."

Paul D. Gibson

San Francisco, CA • 415.822.8087
www.pdgarts.com

TEMPLE VASE 1351. Oil on canvas. 36" x 24"

"My current work is the result of research and influence from the Asian art community, with specific creative problems of contrast in the work, white to black. Venue: Andrea Schwartz Gallery, George Krevsky Gallery.

Keith Grace

Rockford, IL • 815.637.2681
www.grace-design.com

BOSTON PUP. Mixed media. 36" x 48"

"My multi-layered pieces combine collage, acrylic, and oils into seamless, mixed media paintings.
I blend strong visuals with the beauty and power of typography. The words may appear to help
tell the story, but the fragmented pieces are there only to add depth, texture, and balance—
leaving viewers to their own personal interpretation."

Gwendolyn Graine

Falls Church, VA • 703.548.0047
graineart@aol.com

GEOMETRIC. Acrylic, collage. 23" x 19"

"My work is about the interplay between shapes and color. I create my own ordered formalism
by combining a classic sense of order and proportion with the contemporary penchant
for bold expression. The resulting pieces are freeform patchworks of vibrant color."
Venues: Torpedo Factory Art Center Studio, The Art League Gallery, ArtSeen, Inc.

Louis Grant

New York, NY • 212.410.1350
www.lougrantpainting.com

LOOKING AT THE THIRD ONE. Oil on canvas. 40" x 30"

"There is a saying, usually applied to batters in crucial ball and strike situations: 'If it's close enough to look at, it certainly is close enough to swing at!' This painting pictures my recollection of those circumstances. Memories like this one from my days as a young baseball player and fan form the basis of my work." Venues: Frank J. Miele Gallery, George Krevsky Gallery.

David E. Griffin

Broomfield, CO • 303.465.6168
griffin_arts@msn.com

STUDY IN BLUE AND GOLD. Acrylic on canvas. 50" x 62"

"In this piece I used physical layers, an open format, and negative space to describe a contemplative scene from nature while suggesting subtler levels of existence, from the emotional and energetic to the spiritual and existential. I believe art should challenge as well as comfort." Venue: Sandra Phillips Gallery.

Christos Hamawi

Boston, MA • 617.653.7044
www.bluebrickstudios.com

URBAN WILDS. Oil on canvas. 38" x 50"

"A patch of weeds along a busy road, on a city sidewalk, or in an urban park is something that often escapes attention, yet close up these landscapes command awareness and illustrate a foreign world of random shapes, bold colors, varied textures, and beautiful patterns. These types of natural distractions are a major inspiration in my *Nature* series."
Venues: South End Open Studios, SoWa Art Walk.

Marc Ellen Hamel

San Francisco, CA • 415.643.7814
www.marcellenhamel.net

A DAY AT THE LAKE. Oil on canvas. 50" x 46"

"Color is my primary catalyst in making a painting, but the 'story behind the eyes' is crucial to the final image. While applying layers of color, making marks, creating forms within color fields, the artist is constantly reflecting on her experiences, and the finished work becomes a shared story."

Ed Hamilton

Portland, OR • 503.232.3460
www.edhamiltonphoto.com

FRENCH PONIES. Archival inkjet print. 11" x 16.5"

"Mystery of place, solitude, and a heightened sense of nature of things are what matter most to me. These ponies were magical, sentient beings—interested in me as I was in them—informing me of realities yet undiscovered."

Wade Harb

San Diego, CA • 858.243.4640
www.wadeharb.com

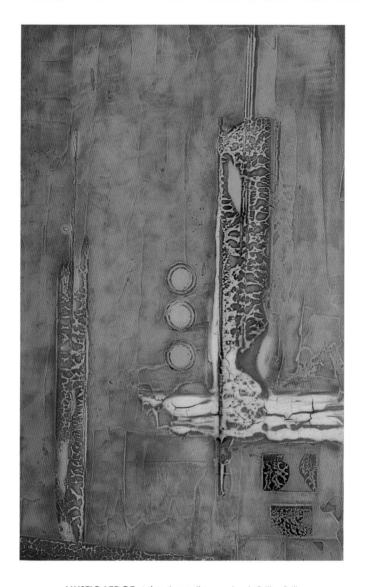

MYSTIC LEDGE. Mixed media on steel. 36" x 24"

"The place I work is without time and filled with agony, frustration, dissonance, and frenzy. And when the spirits will, the outcome is a certain peace. Sharing a glimpse of where I have been is truly magical."

Alice Harrison

Sparta, NJ • 973.726.5960
www.alicenharrison.com

PIECES FOR PEACE 7. Oil with mixed media collage. 31" x 23"

"My inspiration for the series *Pieces for Peace* springs from both personal and social concerns. The dancers in jubilant flight in these collages speak to a deeply felt wish of mine to build a peaceful world. In addition, my work is inspired by the various materials I have collected, as well as by traditional materials in my studio. I work in layers—technically, intellectually, and spiritually— to create images and sensations of movement, color, harmony, and joy."

C. Ellen Hart

Houston, TX • 713.861.2405
www.ellenhartstudios.com

RIVER SHADOW. Acrylic and oil on canvas. 42" x 52"

"My paintings investigate patterns of light and shadow that we experience daily, but that we rarely notice. The works reflect a perceptual duality: a tangible, distinct moment and place when the source pattern is found, intertwined with the fleeting and ephemeral nature of time as shifting light causes my source patterns to move and change." Venue: Buchanan Gallery.

Sherman Hay

Sonora, CA • 209.533.2776
http://home.jps.net/~schay

RAINBOW'S END. Acrylic on canvas. 48" x 36"

"When I start a painting I have a general idea of what I am going to do, that is to follow the path of discovery of shapes, forms, and colors to define the mental atmosphere I am seeking. I try to use universal visual symbols to enable the viewers to trigger the collective unconscious part of our minds. I like this approach because it widens the scope of communication. Prints are available."
Venues: L'Attitude Gallery, Ventana.

Karen Z. Haynes

Arvada, CO • 303.908.7511
www.karenzhaynes.com

HUSH. Oil on panel. 40" x 40"

"*Hush* is part of a series in which I have explored contradictions. This painting looks at vulnerability and strength and uses primitive marks and lines juxtaposed with handwriting. My goal is to use composition, color, and texture to create a compelling and beautiful surface."
Venues: Exhibitrek Gallery, Soren Christensen Gallery, Water Street Gallery.

Tom Heid

El Sobrante, CA • 510.222.9617
www.tomheid.com

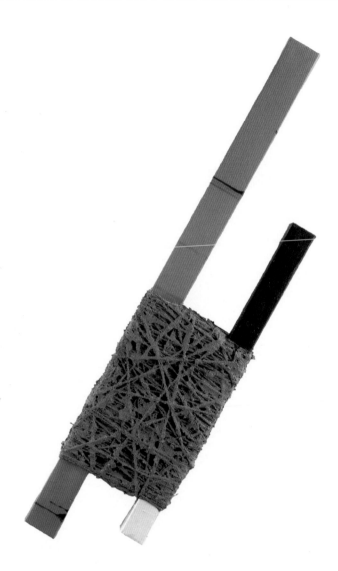

AMERICAN BOUND. Mixed media on canvas. 48" x 10"

"The *Bound* series is my reflection of our unchecked overt consumerism as a nation. Our clamor for inexpensive goods has sent corporate America to other countries where they are able to exploit lax rules involving labor and environmental protection. By using ash and trash in an acrylic polymer emulsion, I hope to convey the eventual breakdown of world resources and destruction of the ecosystem."

Colleen Paul Hoerner

Niwot, CO
www.colleenhoernerpastels.com

PIGEONS OF THE PILLARS. Pastel on paper. 20" x 31"

"I discovered pastel in 1996 and found my love of this wonderfully versatile and vibrant medium. As a contemporary realist, I hope to share my perception of the beauty around us, which I find sometimes in unusual, unnoticed places." Venues: The Great Indoors, Blue Horse Fine Art, Boulder Open Studios.

Bonnie Hofkin

Larkspur, CA • 415.924.3524
www.hofkin.com

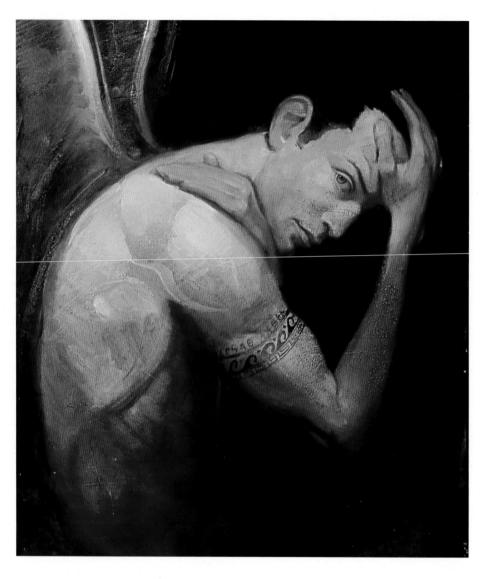

ANGEL. Oil. 24" x 16"

"I'm drawn toward portraiture and thrill at the idea of staging my current interests with a backdrop from my past." Venue: Timmons Gallery, Evolving Art Gallery.

Annie Horkan

Santa Fe, NM • 888.925.4474
www. studiobliss.com

SHE SINGS TO THE COYOTES. Waterbase oil on canvas. 48" x 48"

"*She Sings to the Coyotes* was born from a real life encounter with five coyotes one afternoon in late October on a mesa in the high desert of New Mexico. I did in fact sing to the coyotes. An entire series of paintings called *Tribute to Venus* came to fruition from this trusted feminine response. The coyotes must have wanted more of my singing for they came and hovered around my home for several weeks after our encounter." Venues: Ward-Nasse Gallery, Alex Gallery.

Kimberly Iaconetti

Sausalito, CA • 415.258.8155
keistudios@aol.com

EYE TO EYE. Drawing with watercolor wash. 22" x 15"

"One of the constants when working from life is the quiet transfer of emotion from model to artist. This piece represents that experience along with my passion for strength and sensitivity in drawing, simplicity of line and composition, and capturing the essence of my subject." Venues: Artisans Gallery, Industrial Center Building, Marin Arts Council.

Martine Jardel

San Francisco, CA • 415.921.4823
www.martinejardel.com

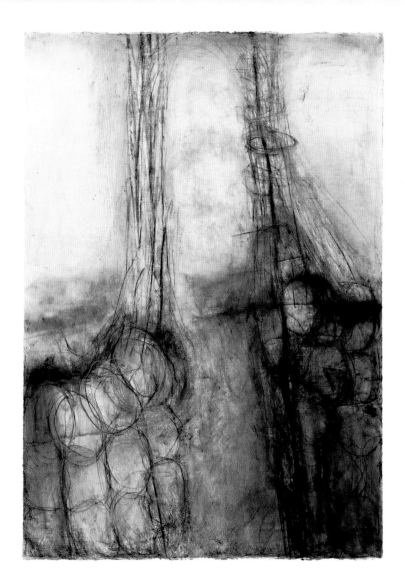

RITE # 20. Charcoal and pastel drawing on paper. 40" x 30"

"Drawing is immediate—a burst of laughter or a burst of tears. The hand rushes fast across the paper retrieving lines and shapes from the primordial soup. Are these signs of unknown wordless languages? Am I re-enacting forgotten rituals? The marks are familiar and yet I know nothing."
Venues: San Francisco Open Studios, Micaëla Gallery.

Diana Johnson

Freeport, ME • 207.865.0583
www.dgjpaint.com

GOLDEN MEADOW. Pastel on sanded paper. 10" x 16"

"I create vibrant, harmonious paintings that provide visual places of rest and rejuvenation. The rhythmic, fluid effects of radiant energy on landscapes inspire me. The more a painting seems to emit luminosity, as if from the paper itself, the happier I am with the results." Venues: Fore Street Gallery, Little Sebago Gallery, Sebascodegan Gallery.

Eric Joyner

San Francisco, CA • 415.305.3992
www.ericjoyner.com

THE INTERRUPTION. Oil on wood panel. 16" x 20"

"This painting is a statement about government intrusion and annoying beings in general. The donut-holding robot just wants a peaceful moment but is interrupted. On top of this, he is told the donut is bad for him and he should not eat it. What's a metal-man to do?"

GILLETTE'S BRIDGE. Mixed media on paper. 42" x 38"

"I look at art as a process of self-discovery and salvation, and I choose to focus on
what is positive and beautiful within those discoveries. It is never a question as to what
the work is about, it is always a presence of the hand and mind, soul and color."
Venues: ArtReach, Erdreich White Fine Art.

Ronna Katz

Albuquerque, NM • 505.480.0442
ronnaonthewall@hotmail.com

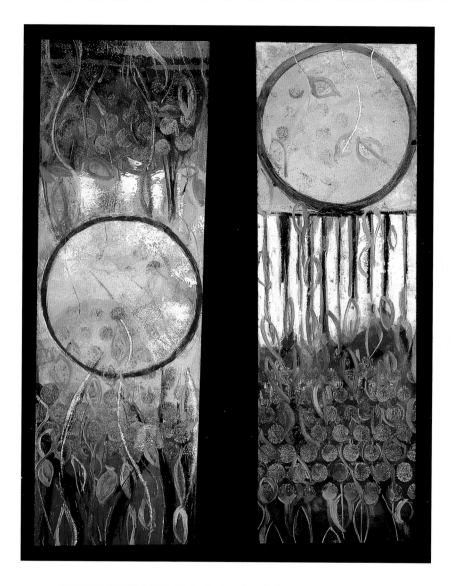

MYSTERY IN THE QUIET. Diptych. Acrylic, oil, ink on paper. 38" x 18"

"I focus on painting abstracts and my work is inspired by nature, quite often incorporating symbols and organic elements. I mostly paint with oil-based inks and paints on primed paper, coarse linen, and recently have been exploring the textured panel surface."

Ivan Kende

Toledo, OH • 419.474.7945
www.ivankende.com

GODDESS OF BLUE. Acrylic on canvas. 36" x 30"

"In this work, using my preferred technique of layers of controlled texture and mono-
chromatic color theme, I sought to paint my vision of the elemental feminine energy
which creates form from the formless, the recognizable from the abstract."
Venues: Chelsea Gallery, The Tom James Gallery.

James Kinny

Boston, MA • 617 312.5126
jameskinnyart@aol.com

J0602. Acrylic on canvas. 18" x 18"

"Painting is like having a conversation with a stranger. I speak. The painting speaks. I respond, the painting responds. We take many breaks to think about what's been said. We revisit many times. In this spontaneous method of painting, the history of the conversation is ever present on the canvas." Venues: Nielsen Gallery, Gallery Merz, Bernard Toale Gallery.

Jamie Kirkland

Santa Fe, NM • 801.520.2410
www.jamiekirklandart.com

TO THE WEST. Oil on canvas. 48" x 60"

"My painting is about capturing a feeling of natural stillness and tranquility through transmutation of paint into lyrical expressions of color and mood. I have always been moved by Iris Murdoch's description of the artistic process: 'Artists dream of a silence which they must enter as some creatures return to the sea to spawn.' I aspire to convey the transcendent pleasure derived from the experience of painting." Venues: Winterowd Fine Art, Phoenix Gallery, g2 Gallery.

Jennifer Kirton

Mount Dora, FL • 407.889.5437
kirtonart@aol.com

PAT'S ROSES. Drawing. 14" x 10"

"Intrigued with the joy of drawing, I love pushing the limits of the media. Contrast, value, tone, shape, and composition are constant challenges making each rendering take on its own distinctive and unique character. All work is original and inspired by my surroundings and imagination."

Casey Klahn

Davenport, WA • 509.796.3277
www.fineartstudioonline.com/caseyklahn

HILL WITH RED SKY. Pastel on board. 12.5" x 9.5"

"The motif of the landscape is incidental to me when the subject is the indescribable beauty and impact of color." Venues: Bellevue Artsfair, Park City Art Festival, Sun Valley Arts & Crafts Festival.

Marsha Klein

Sonoma, CA • 707.935.1207
www.marshaklein.com

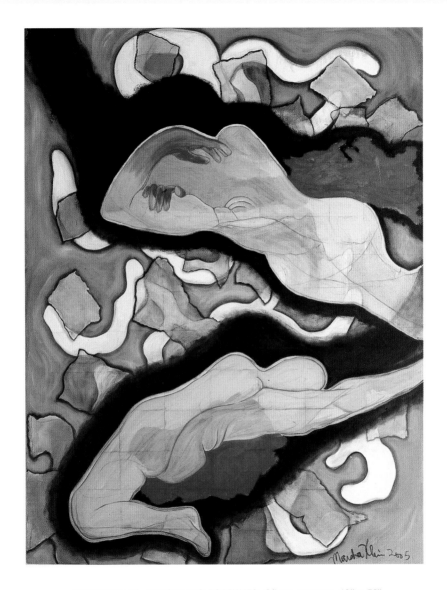

DREAMERS #4, UNFOLDING FORTUNES. Oil on canvas. 68" x 52"

"Disembodied rib bones and chance windows of translucent fortunes are carried on turbulent winds of a wildly fluctuating time. The dreamers—cocooned in shadows—hang suspended with the presence of passion and the veil of physical reality."

MEANDERING. Acrylic on canvas. 27" x 18"

"I am inspired by the quality of light, atmosphere, and mood in my landscapes, which I usually begin *en plein air*. I am especially drawn to the intimate view, and to express a sense of mystery and beauty in otherwise ordinary places and overlooked subjects." Venues: Chesapeake Gallery, American Painting Gallery.

Kevan Krasnoff

Boulder, CO • 303.444.0693
k_krasnoff@hotmail.com

OPAL. Acrylic on canvas. 52" x 40"

"Painting from my imagination and life experiences offers infinite possibilities. I don't paint with the assumption of 'finished,' rather with the relationship to timeless evolution and re-evaluation of time, place, and situation. I don't know what I will paint today, or tomorrow, but I probably will paint." Venues: Arte Misia Gallery, Anderson O'Brien Fine Art, Lumina Contemporary Art.

Darlene Kuhne

Boulder, CO • 720.935.2596
bdjsinc@earthlink.net

SILVER LINING. Acrylic on paper. 24" x 32"

"Colors, shapes, and lines emerge to capture, entwine, and bounce around the picture plane.
My paintings are multi-layered, splattered, dotted, and squiggled for texture and depth."
Venues: New York Art Expo, Las Vegas Expo, Chicago Neocon.

Kathleen Lack

Novato, CA • 415.883.5363
www.kathleenlack.com

WAITING FOR THE DANCE. Oil on canvas. 40" x 30"

When Olivia settled into her pose for the day, I immediately was presented with another compelling reason to paint. Figures are my inspiration. Color is my passion. Emotion is my glue."
Venues: Lyons Head Gallery, Marin Art Festival, Marin Open Studios.

Barbara Lawrence

Forest Knolls, CA • 415.488.1436
www.bl4art.com

CALIFORNIA POPPIES. Oil on canvas. 12" x 12"

"This painting is more fantasy than reality. As I grow, I become freer to express, creating my vision, opening my inner window. I teach a two-week workshop, yearly, in southern France." Venues: Robert Allen Fine Arts, Marin Scapes, Mill Valley Fall Arts Festival.

Beatriz Ledesma

Chicago, IL • 773.561.0825
www.ledesmastudio.com

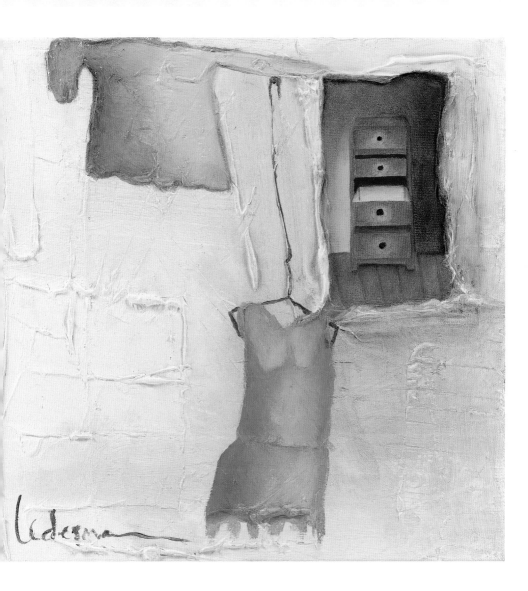

MYSTERIOUS DRESSER. Oil on canvas. 12" x 12"

"My work is informed by mysticism, spirituality, dreams, and psychoanalysis, and the work of surrealist painters with the interest to manifest the unconscious through the art-making process. *Mysterious Dresser* is part of the *Windows* series, a painted reflection on inner and outer worlds, and the impact that one has upon the other." Venues: Chicago City Arts Gallery, Women Made Gallery, Around the Coyote Gallery.

Freda Lee-McCann

Columbia, MD • 410.381.3499
www.fredalee.com

ENLIGHTENED. Watercolor. 30" x 22"

"Mountains, the bones of the earth, have been my favorite subject for painting. I love the brushwork that is unique to the Chinese painting tradition. I painted this work by using watercolor to do the brush strokes instead of ink. It freed me to express my emotions in a unique way while still retaining the traditional Chinese character in the work."

Rusty Leffel

Mission Hills, KS • 913 362 9727
rcleffel@aol.com

WAR TOYS. Photograph. 11" x 14"

"My work is street photography. I am fascinated by cities and the way we live our daily lives in them. Artistically, I look for how we interact with each other and with the built environment around us. Photographs are on film, scanned digitally, and printed sepia-toned on archival papers."

Jorge Leyva

Joplin, MO • 417.483.9490
www.odysseastudio.com

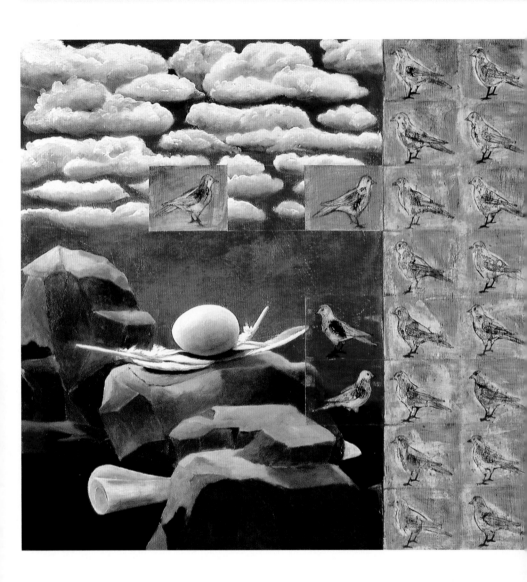

THE BIRD ARCHITECT. Mixed media on panel. 54" x 58"

"Nature with all its elements and creatures inspires me."
Venues: NuArt Gallery, Daum Museum of Contemporary Art.

Lisette T. Lichtenstein

Columbus, OH • 614.888.8284
www.lisettelichtenstein.com

PINK. Encaustic on panel. 48" x 48"

"My paintings are a body of changing ideas with a focus on form, color, and composition, illusion, and the question of beauty, figurative versus abstract, motion, and texture. I am working toward an honest and serious expression of art, searching out themes of society to satisfy our needs for visual nourishment and excitement."

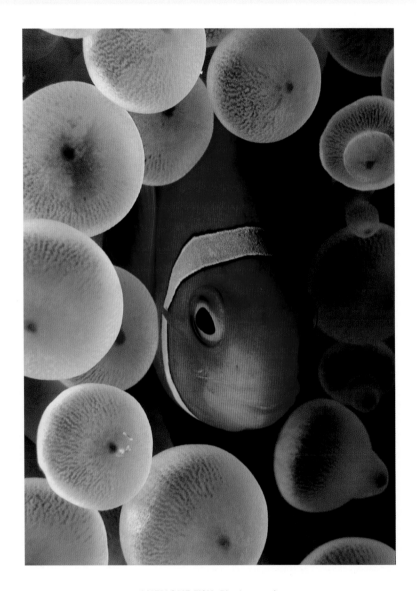

ANEMONE FISH. Photograph

"This underwater photograph captures the tiny but intense face of an anemone fish in its host anemone. I spent numerous dives visiting this anemone to try and get just the right moment and composition. This image was created in the Solomon Islands." Venue: Coastal Arts League, Frame Circus.

Cal Ling

Chico, CA • 530.893.0882
cling@shocking.com

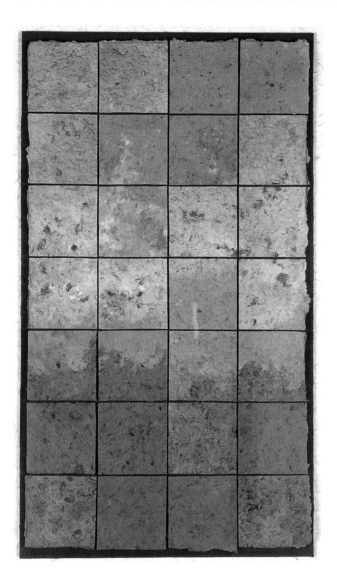

HEAVENLY BAMBOO. Handmade paper on silk. 38" x 25"

"Translating with color, light, and texture memories and moments that fill us up. My work is a dialogue of inner and outer influences that transforms itself into a visual dialogue with myself and the viewer. It is visual poetry of the spirit that keeps us all in balance."
Venues: Diseno Verde, Our House, Options.

SHE WINTERS AND KEEPS WARM. Pastel on metallic gouache. 24" x 18"

"I have an intense concern for detail and a passion for the underlying line, mirroring the emotions and attitudes of my subjects, going beyond the surface to express intimate feelings and states of mind. *She Winters and Keeps Warm* is part of a new series, *Burnished Metal*." Venues: Amsterdam Whitney Gallery, Artisans Art Gallery.

Carol Lopatin

Alexandria, VA • 703.683.3535
www.carollopatin.com

NEFF'S CANYON. Acrylic on paper. 30" x 22"

"Painting with acrylics on location in the clear air above Salt Lake City, I began with the sky and continued to explore 'place.' My style is fluid and interpretive. Final decisions regarding composition and paint quality are made in the studio." Venues: Mark Palmer Gallery, Strathmore Arts Center, Oxford Fine Arts Fair.

Ann Luce

Boulder, CO • 303.443.9039
aluce67004@aol.com

SAN MIGUEL MADONNA. Oil on canvas. 30" x 24"

"The human figure speaks its own language. The curve of a person's back, shoulders, hands, and face seem to speak about his or her inner thoughts, fears, worries, peace, and even joys. They tell stories. The *San Miguel Madonna* was painted from a sketch I did in front of the cathedral."
Venue: Alarion Gallery.

Ed Lucey

Los Gatos, CA
elucey41@verizon.net

ALONG WEST ROAD. Acrylic on canvas. 30" x 40"

"I prefer the *alla prima* method of painting showing a lot of brushwork. California countryside and urban landscapes make up the largest part of my work. This scene is taken from the area west of Healdsburg, California."

Susan Lynn

Kansas City, MO • 816.765.7841
www.susanlynnwatercolors.com

SUNLIT CORN. Watercolor on paper. 7" x 10"

"Using heightened, abstracted color, my paintings explore the landscape of the Great Plains and the American West. Incorporating the luminous quality of transparent watercolor, I paint with intense, saturated colors, creating color and textural transitions that echo those found in nature." Venues: The Phoenix Gallery, The Rice Gallery.

Debra Maddox

Mill Valley, CA • 415.846.5100
www.debramaddoxfineart.com

CARIBBEAN SWIMMER. Photography and oil on canvas. 20" x 20"

"Documenting the perceptual environment either through painting or photography has always intrigued me. I have devised a method of combining the two media blurring the boundaries between painting and photography." Venues: Sausalito Art Festival, Marin Open Studios.

Jeffrey Majer

Richmond, VA • 804.874.4350
www.jeffreymajer.com

MOTHERS or **BICNIC**. Acrylic and enamels on panel. 4' x 4'

"Much of art deals with sadness, heartache, and tragedy. My *Mother and Child* series looks at the most powerful type of love. Interested in the bonds in Cassatt's paintings, I was never taken by her handling. I contrast the sensitive interaction with a direct paint application."
Venue: ADA Gallery.

Stela Mandel

Greenbrae, CA • 415.461.9159
www.stelamandel.com

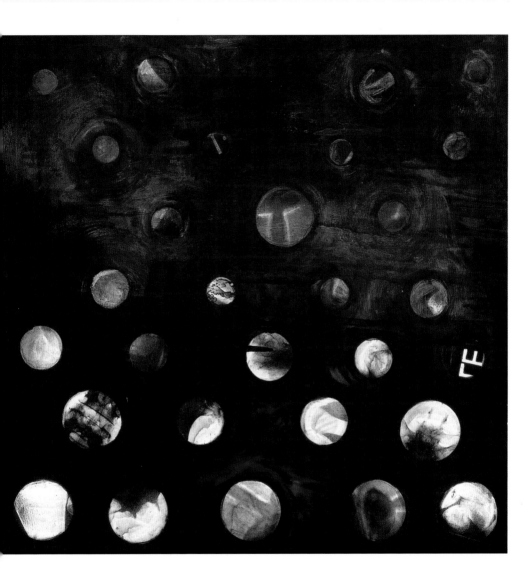

PIE IN THE SKY. X-rays, oil, acrylics on canvas. 30" x 30"

"My recent work combines the medical imagery that I have worked with over the last six years with other visual devices. In *Pie in the Sky* I used the pie chart to structure x-ray photos into a composition. The interplay of unrelated content is what interests and drives me."
Venues: California Modern Gallery, Marin Open Studios.

Anne Marchand

Washington, DC • 202.265.5882
www.annemarchand.com

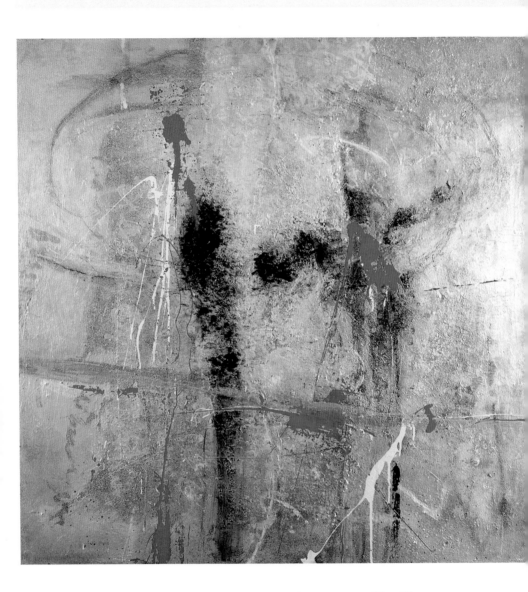

UNTITLED #1. Acrylic, mixed media on canvas. 48" x 48"

"Energy surrounds us at every level in the universe. In this work, I am celebrating the dance of life with all its mysteries. *Untitled #1* takes a new vantage point of spontaneous play. It leads into my newest series of paintings called *Leela*." Venues: Zenith Galley, Joe Wilcox Fine Arts, Arches Gallery.

David S. Mark

San Francisco, CA • 415.239.0230
www.markresourceusa.com

REQUIEM FOR LIFE'S PERSISTENCE. Oil on wood. 3' x 4'

"Life emerged in our world challenged by numerous natural catastrophes, and proclaimed its tenacity repeatedly in the face of near total mass extinction of living species. Life's persistence, pitted against a continuously changing environment, both natural and human-generated, serves as a major facet of my work, and addresses a deepening understanding of earth processes in the sustainability of life." Venues: Evolving Art Gallery, SFMOMA Artists Gallery, JFK Video Installation.

WINTER WITH A YELLOW CAT. Acrylic on canvas. 48" x 58"

"After we moved to Missouri, our three dogs and three cats were always close at hand in their new home. The yellow cat is pretty close to annoying, but he loves the warmth of the dogs and me and can't help but be in any space I am in."

Nicholas Mathios

Belleair, FL • 727.461.9155
www.artbymathios.com

CURIOUS. Acrylic on canvas. 20" x 20"

"I found *Curious* in the village of Oia on the island of Santorini and painted her on my return to Florida. Although the majority of my work is landscapes, here and abroad, I am devoting more time to the human figure and find *Curious* an ideal study." Venues: Dunedin Fine Art Center, Leeper Rattner Museum Bookstore.

Scott Matyjaszek

Rochester, NY • 585.254.1380
www.artephax.com

TOUCH. Photograph. 28" x 42"

"I photographed this rock formation in Lower Antelope Canyon near Lake Powell in
Northern Arizona. The movement is sensual, and the evocative shapes have a feminine quality."
Venues: Columbus Arts Festival, South University Art Fair.

GUANAJUATO 4. Monotype. 30" x 20.5"

"I alternate between painting and printmaking several times a year, sometimes working on a series of monotypes to try out a new idea. On a recent trip to Mexico, I felt so saturated with the warm and colorful surroundings, the history, the people, art, and architecture. My visions of the walls especially symbolize for me everything I experienced there, and I have worked through monotypes to recreate my memory of the trip ever since."

Clem McCarthy

Sausalito, CA • 415.331.1560
www.clemmccarthy.com

WEST L.A. Oil on canvas. 24" x 20"

"Part of my job as an advertising director was scouting locations, and I always made sure to carry a sketch pad along with me. Los Angeles—with its diverse neighborhoods and wonderful light—provided good fodder for the canvas."

Peter Leone McCormick

San Francisco, CA • 415.928.7779
petermccormick@earthlink.net

REFUGE. Paper collage. 11" x 7.5"

"My work is a dialogue between the natural beauty of the materials and my subconscious transformed into metaphor and symbol. I immerse in play that is experimental and invigorating to my curiosity. I always discover."

Gale S. McKee

San Rafael, CA • 415.459.2981
galesmckee@comcast.net

THE TELLTALE. Acrylic on canvas and boat sails. 58" x 54"

"The style of my monumental paintings is Abstract Expressionistic. I paint on boat sails that have been reconstructed in unique and unexpected ways. I use the inherent geometric designs and improvise with acrylic color, shape, texture, and nautical salvage. They are the abstract 'essence' of sailing."

THOUGHT #22. Acrylic and ink on canvas. 48" x 34"

"Thoughts is a series reflecting my passion for flight. Lines suggest ambiguous spatial effects, and the colors' luminance offers momentary perceptions of flotation and movement."

Maralyn Miller

Los Gatos, CA • 408.354.6747
www.maralynmillerstudio.com

FORGOTTEN BARN. Pastel on paper. 16" x 20"

"This is one of the scenes I painted because it represents the California farms of the past.
They are becoming scarce as urban sprawl takes over." Venues: Stone Griffin Gallery,
Valley Art Gallery, Casa Galleria.

Bonnie Mineo

Boston, MA • 617.428.3735
www.bonniemineo.com

CANYON SYMMETRY. Relief print. 23" x 13"

"The afternoon fades gently...This series of unique prints are impressions of places I have traveled through, building on memories of light and form, color and contrast. Using simple foam plates, printing and overprinting with transparent inks, I evoke the chromatic character of 'moments' in textures and abstract forms." Venues: Fort Point Open Studios, Jacqueline Becker Fine Arts Consulting, Louisa Gould Gallery.

Catherine Molland

Santa Fe, NM • 505.983.1909
www.catherinemolland.com

AFRICAN QUEEN. Oil on canvas. 36" x 48"

"My art grows out of a reverence for the mysterious wonder of nature. Earth rhythms like the moon's phases and the seasons' cycles of birth, growth, death, and rebirth fascinate me. The people I paint are often archetypes of these elemental forces. Beauty is a primal force, always inspiring."

Melanie Moore

Las Vegas, NV • 312.226.3745
mmoore7@mindspring.com

CHICAGO MEMORIES. Mixed media on canvas. 30" x 40"

"*Chicago Memories* reflects my memory of Chicago—the energy of the people and the incredible architecture, combined to create the feeling of the city. Several images fit together to tell the story, not representing life as it actually is, but representing life as a memory."
Venue: Caconline.org.

Mitsuyo Moore

Oakland, CA • 510.633.9327
www.mitsuyomoore.com

HONORING YOUR INNER LIGHT. Acrylic and coarse pumice gel on canvas. 48" x 36"

"Line is the most basic element of vision, as it reveals rhythm, movement, and spirituality. Color enhances the vision and also stimulates emotions. The light in you, a source of tremendous strength in daily life, produces gentle yet very positive energy. I believe that our happiness can be found seeking it within ourselves and not in others."

Larry Morace

San Francisco, CA • 415.759.5755
www.moraceart.com

CITY CANYON #8. Oil on canvas. 68" x 52"

"These urban canyons offer up such orderly geometry, it seems a painting would be easy to put together. Once into the drawing, however, I face a dizziness of decision, as Kierkegaard says, with too many choices. I find myself quickly improvising. Drawing, it demands thinking on my feet—it never gets old." Venues: Newmark Gallery, Chemers Gallery.

Catherine Moreno

Mill Valley, CA • 415.388.0822
www.cathmoreno.com

SANDBANK. Oil on panel 12" x 14"

"Here is a microecology—tide changing a tiny bulwark of sandy earth. Water has a profundity and mystery I love to ponder and depict: its swirling, graceful impermanent geometries, its endless play with light and reflections, its awesome force in creating, sustaining, and destroying." Venues: Marin Open Studios, Marin Society of Artists, San Francisco Women Artists.

Katherine Morgan

Boca Raton, FL • 561.241.0064
www.kmaphotos.com

ELEMENTS. Photograph. 24" x 16"

"As a photographer, I strive to evoke my freedom to observe. I select each image that embraces me in the moment with a touch of humor, serenity, beauty, history, emotion, intrigue, or whimsy. I capture and freeze the moment in time, knowing with each one I have been gifted...once."
Venues: Boca Raton Museum of Art, Aquarian Age Gallery, Meyerhoefer Gallery.

M. Morgan

California • 408.242.6967
www.mmorganphotography.com

GOLDEN GATE FROM THE PRESIDIO. Photograph. 22" x 28"

"Finding a new point of view in this vastly photographed world is our mission. This image typifies our style: infrared black and white with partial colorization. Our alternate processes and unique perspective of the bridge often challenge viewers to accept this as a single image captured on film."

142

Marilyn M. Mull

Boulder, CO
marilynmull@comcast.net

MEXICAN HIBISCUS. Medium and soft pastels on sanded paper. 21" x 30"

"This image is a 'bee's eye view' of a large colorful red and yellow hibiscus blossom that I saw at Hacienda San Gabriel de Barrera on a recent winter trip to Guanajuato, Mexico."

Dan Neuberger

Rochester, NY • 585.482.1976
www.imagecityphotographygallery.com

BLUE ROOM. Archival digital print

"Sometimes it pays to be nice. I was helping a friend by doing some still shots for her film, and during down time, I wandered around the old armory where the film was being shot, and *voila*, I discovered this enchanting blue room!" Venues: Image City Photography Gallery, Michael Banzhaf Gallery, The Camera Obscura Gallery.

Lynda Newell

Novato, CA • 415.595.5471
www.lyndanewell.com

REFLECTIONS. Acrylic on canvas. 24" x 20"

"My paintings are abstracted from natural objects. I use shapes and surface texture to create visual metaphors for contemporary life. *Reflections* is the result of an intuitive exploration of color, line, shape, and texture. Using palette knives and thin acrylic glazes, I watch the parts come alive in the process of surrender and exploration." Venues: North Bay Art Works, Marin Open Studios.

THE KORAI SERIES: RED CARPET (GOLD). Oil. 48" x 36"

"I was out walking on a moonless night. As I crossed the street, my attention was drawn to a shop window. I stopped in front of the window. The interior was flooded with gleaming light. A mannequin stood there elegantly poised, a vision of the goddess encapsulated in glass."

Connie Noyes

Chicago, IL • 415.299.1754
www.connienoyes.com

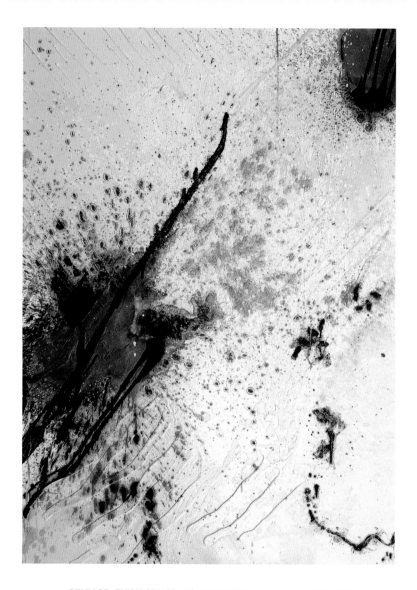

RELEASE, FLESH SERIES. Mixed media on canvas. 48" x 36"

"What began innocently as a tender whisper of love, ended in a scream of terror.
Such is the beginning of life and its contradictions." Venues: Bill Lowe Gallery, Select Art,
Art Services International.

BLUE CENTER 1. Oil on canvas. 50" x 50"

"This piece falls in the photorealist vein with some romantic license taken with regard to color and emphasis. The red tulips grow in my garden and take on wonderful symbolic qualities when I blow them up to a large scale. The reflections and distortions in the hand-made glass lend a mystical, whimsical air to the implied importance of the work." Venues: Jain Marunouchi Gallery, Maryland Art Place, National Museum of Women in the Arts.

Hanya Popova Parker

Santa Rosa, CA • 707.527.5447
www.hanyapopovaparker.com

LAGUNA WILDLIFE. Oil on canvas. 24" x 24"

"I painted this to donate for an annual fundraiser for the Laguna de Santa Rosa Foundation of Sonoma County, which is one of my favorite non-profits. I was intrigued by the abstract quality of the water and surroundings while also fascinated by the late evening color."

Joan Parker

Westwood, KS • 913.384.0617
www.joanparkerfineart.com

100 YEAR OLD QUAKER CHURCH. Oil on canvas. 12" x 24"

"My intent is to concentrate on the history and spaces between and around the farms in the Flint Hills of Kansas, revealing what is there. The land, the people's history, and the light."
Venues: KA Masters Art Show at Strecker-Nelson Gallery, Pasadena Art Museum, Kodner Gallery.

Sharon Paster

Kentfield, CA • 415.457.8671
thepasters@earthlink.net

WEST MARIN. Oil on wood panel. 35" x 42"

"My goal is to reflect the 'state of possibility.' Everything in the atmosphere vibrates with life, on the verge of movement and change, and nothing expresses this more than the ocean rushing against the beach. I paint over textured areas, scribble onto the surface, and aim to capture the moment through gestural brushstroke and line."

Mike Pavol

Philadelphia, PA • 215.990.2973
www.mikepavol.com

MARCH WITH SPEARS/OCCUPATION. Oil on canvas. 10' 2" x 9' 9"

"In the past year I have continued exploring the potential of low-tone painting and looked further into figurative work and ambi-narrative presentation. Executing these works at a large size and with multiple panels such as in *March with Spears/Occupation*, allows the work to approach an environmental and architectural realm while conveying illustrative and aesthetic information. This low-tone work is adjusted for printing limitations, and is a suggestion of the actual work."

Virginia Pendergrass

Brevard, NC • 828.885.5147
www.home.earthlink.net/~vependergr

MIST ON THE RIVER. Oil on canvas board. 20" x 16"

"*Mist on the River* was painted *en plein air* in the North Carolina mountains. I wanted to capture the mysterious, dream-like quality of the misty day. In keeping with contemporary impressionism, I strive for exuberant color, loose brushwork, and semi-abstract forms." Venues: Bluewood Gallery, Red Clover Gallery, Silver Fox Gallery.

BIRDSONG. Oil on canvas. 24" x 18"

"I am interested in symbolism and metaphor, ceremony and ritual. I want to explore the connection between man and nature with a sense of mythology. I want my eyes to be open to life—to be conscious of the subtleties and wonderment. This is the foundation my work is built upon."

Gina Pierleoni

Bel Air, MD • 410.836.2546
www.ginapierleoni.com

48 WEEKS. Acrylic, pastel, and ink on paper. 72" x 51"

"*48 Weeks* refers to the period of time my husband underwent chemotherapy last year, as well as the cycle required to complete this painting. My intention was to create a touchstone for grounding my self and a visual prayer for his recovery. All's well in my world!"
Venues: Maxwell Fine Arts, Peekskill, Spiziri Art Group.

Giraud Polite

Dallas, TX • 214.577.0733
www.giraudpolite.com

OFFERING. Photograph. 20" x 30"

"The exploration of form, line, and rhythm in my photography function as points of departure within my greater pursuit for optimal composition. *Offering* is a part of the festival series *Dance of the Gods*, in which I attempt to illustrate the visual language of a community of Oaxacan Mexicans as they prepare for a La Guelaguetza dance performance."

Nancy Pollock

San Rafael, CA • 415.721.7752
rtcrrtz@aol.com

INTERSECTION. Oil encaustic on wood. 12" x 12"

"The beeswax medium speaks to me. Although the materials and processes date back thousands of years, I find them to be current and relevant. Making encaustic work is both organic and transformative. The beauty of the medium is that it is rigorous and forgiving."

Silvia Poloto

San Francisco, CA • 415.641.5878
www.poloto.com

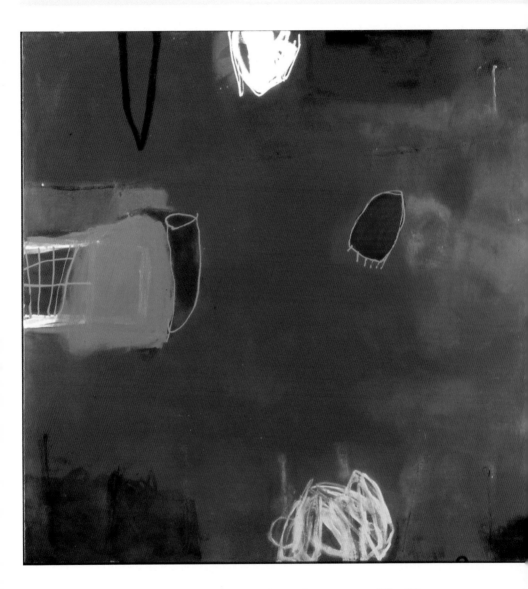

OBSERVATIONS IN DEEP BLUE. Acrylic on canvas. 50" x 50"

"My abstract work is a purely visual endeavor—it has everything to do with the process, which inevitably will express my self and aspirations. This process, which I approach intuitively, seems to open my imagination. It's dynamic, without a predetermined idea—the paintings develop and evolve as I work on them. I let them find what they want to be."
Venues: Toomey Tourell, Butters Gallery, Julie Nester Gallery.

Leo Posillico

Santa Rosa, CA • 707.568.5465
www.posillicostudio.com

IT'S AN UPSCALE NEIGHBORHOOD. Mixed media on canvas. 30" x 40" x 4.5"

"My mixed media paintings use acrylic on canvas with metal, wood, paper, ink, and oil pastels which I form and construct into different series of work such as the *Gallery* series. This series studies the various art works one can be exposed to while in the gallery, both humorous and serious, and how we as viewers interact with the art. This piece shows interior and exterior scenes combined."

METAMORPHOSIS OF FRIDA. Watercolor on paper. 30" x 22"

"*Metamorphosis of Frida* is from a series of abstractions in drawings and paintings using Frida Kahlo as a subject. This is the last of the series, where Frida transforms into a butterfly."

Michael Raaum

Basalt, CO • 970.927.3617
www.michaelraaum.com

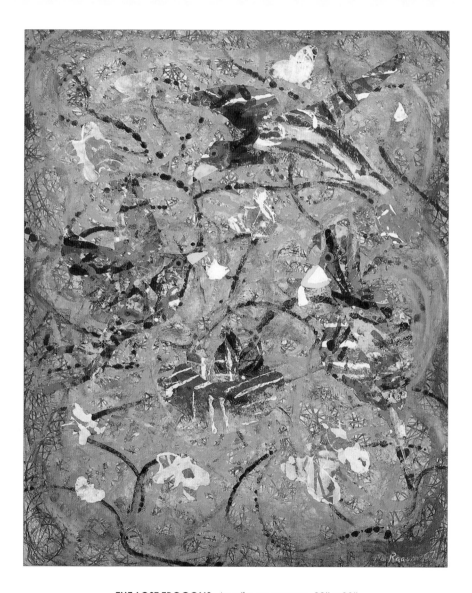

THE LOST TROGONS. Acrylic on canvas. 38" x 30"

"In *The Lost Trogons*, I noticed bird shapes in my automatic marks. Using my subconscious it started without a plan. I then found meaningful relationships with the light blue butterfly shapes. The process was a visual conversation involving ideas, shapes, and colors. This composition reflects my happiness in discovery."

Arlene Reiss

Albion, CA • 707.937.0405
www.partnersgallery.com

ANTIQUITY. Acrylic. 30" x 22"

"My work is abstract and intuitive with no outside frame of reference. I want to leave the door open for others to bring their own visions, experiences, and interpretations to the work. It's fascinating and mysterious that by making marks on paper, a reality is created that never existed before."
Venue: Partners Gallery.

Jonathan Rischawy

Flemington, NJ • 908.237.1939
www.painters-studio.com

BOWMAN'S BRIDGE. Acrylic on canvas. 20" x 16"

"The lighting in a scene is just as important as the subject matter, and in some cases it can be the subject matter. I am also fascinated with man-made structures in nature, such as the century-old barn, the steel truss of a bridge, or a simple farm gate. The juxtaposition of these objects in nature create a wonderfully harmonious contrast."

Christina Roe

Fresno, CA • 559.226.1533
christinaroe@hotmail.com

METROPOLIS III. Painted, cast paper mosaic. 38" x 39"

"I create shapes and textures out of hand-made paper, which is then boldly painted. My artwork usually begins with a clay original, from which a mold is made, and then cast using paper pulp, which I recycle myself. Richly colored and textured, my multi-layered relief surfaces are frequently integrated with collage."

Thierry Rosset

San Francisco, CA • 415.921.4823
www.mesart.com/thierryrosset

BLACK HOLES I. Linocut. 30" x 22"

"Lines are endless and lead to the infinite. On the other hand, shapes define a limited space. I aim at provoking a dialogue (or perhaps a rejection) between both of them. I am intrigued by the tension so created." Venues: The 8 Gallery, San Francisco Open Studios.

J. Luray Schaffner

St. Leonard, MD • 410.586.1652
jlurayschaffner@comcast.net

SEPTEMBER LIGHTS. Mixed media collage. 40" x 30"

"The intensity of color hues of similar value, along with the use of textures, creates a torch of color with waves of light creating a visual line. The repetitive dot pattern balances the harmony of color. I use hand-painted papers, silkscreen fragments with a white translucent wash and color-saturated rice paper." Venues: Torpedo Factory Art Center, Designers Two, CalvART Gallery.

Judy Lyons Schneider

Bradenton, FL • 941.907.2907
www.judyschneider.artspan.com

RAMILAS #1. Monoprint with mixed media. 32" x 25"

"Layer upon layer, color upon color, image upon image—these are the ways my printmaking and mixing media begin. In this piece, using tree branches to draw the viewer in, my work is evocative and personal. The surprise of the layering process is a very exciting one for me. It is what draws me to my etching press over and over." Venues: The Collectors Wall Fine Art Galleries, Art Center Manatee.

Julie Hughes Shabkie

Greenville, SC • 864.233.9340
jshabkie@charter.net

SCOTTISH HIGHLANDS. Mixed media on paper. 18" x 24"

"This work was created after a stay in Scotland. I chose to use both representational and abstract styles to represent the contrasts of beauty and edginess that I experienced in the Highlands, Glasgow, and Edinburgh." Venues: Village Studios and Gallery, Greenville Open Studios.

Sharon Rusch Shaver

Gallatin, TN • 615.451.7304
www.sharonruschshaver.com

THE NEW SONG. Oil on canvas. 24" x 18"

"A simple subject, a well-composed arrangement, an attractive painting, and thought. Ground is becoming less and figure more. Darkness fills less and exquisite color more. It is a subtle transformation and perhaps only temporary; a constant fine tuning of technique and presentation, as well as an ever open eye to new expression." Venue: Michael B. Tusing Gallery.

David Skinner

Venice, CA • 310.399.6649
www.dskinner.net

UP-COUNTRY. Acrylic on canvas. 30" x 30"

"Influenced by the rich legacy of the California *plein air* painters, I go into the field to do sketches and shoot photographs so that I'll remember the light and terrain. Each painting begins with a conceived direction, which then transforms as certain marks and colors influence and guide me."
Venues: McLean Gallery, McRae & Company, Elder Gallery.

Kathleen deFrancesco Smith

Loveland, OH • 513.677.3444
http://kdefsmith.artspan.com

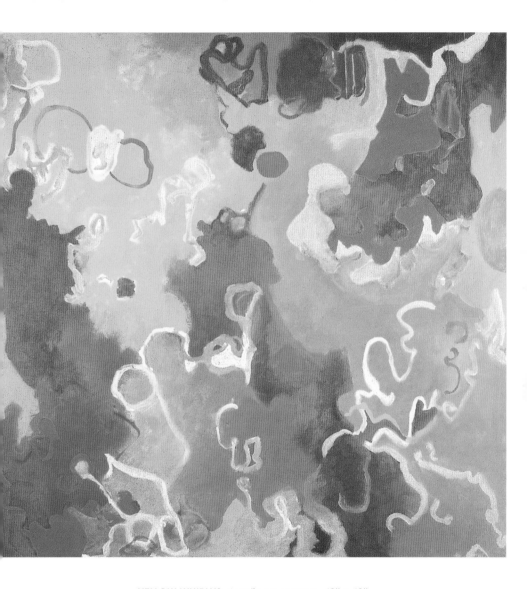

YELLOW WHIRLYS. Acrylic on canvas. 48" x 48"

"I work intuitively, allowing the painting to build itself as I add and subtract color, lines, and shapes. A dialogue with the painting ensues, and I become focused on building images. The lines begin to contour and define edges, confine spaces, and form shapes. Line adds a dimensionality to the airiness of the color field." Venues: Art Design Consultants, Gallery 22.

Lyn Smith

Dubois, WY • 307.455.2204
www.photographydesigns.com

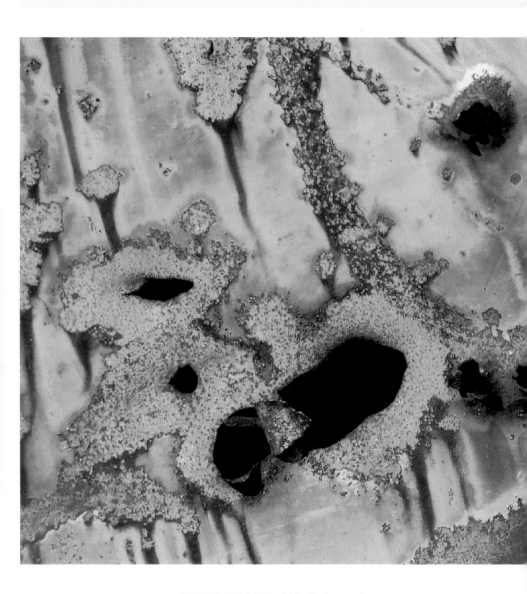

SHOT UP OLD RUSTY CAR. Photograph

"Nature creates the most extraordinary yet simple patterns, some lasting for just brief periods of time, rarely seen before being altered and re-worked by new forces. My photography preserves some of these natural designs, recording the intimacy of the discovery past the composition's sometimes brief existence. Each photograph commemorates the beauty in a simple observance that might otherwise have passed by unnoticed."

Jane Smithers

Cashiers, NC • 828.743.6541
www.janesmithers.com

TREETOPS. Oil on canvas. 24" x 24"

"Each stroke of the palette knife with rich, textured, brilliant oil paints declares my absolute commitment to my art! The endless possibilities afforded by large canvases provide the venue for a wonderful adventure. This is my way of grasping reality and my perpetual quest to know myself."
Venues: Altitude Art Gallery, Flanders Art Gallery, Summit One Gallery.

Linda Spencer

Tavares, FL • 352.343.4044
www.spencerarts.com

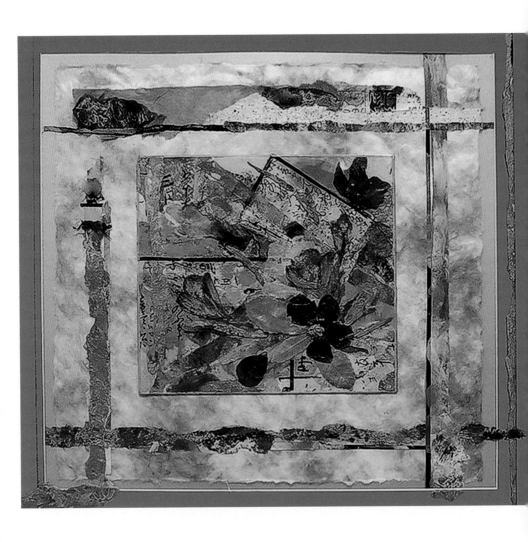

LIFE FLAME. Mixed media. 26" x 28"

"To create this image I used melted beeswax, resin, and pigment. A Japanese *shikishi* board is pressed into the paint. Next I use hand-made papers, flower parts, and tree bark to create layers of interest. After the work is dry, I mount and embellish it. The layered mat work protects the plants that rise up from the paint and it gives the work dimension."

Jeri Spressart

Annapolis, MD • 410.757.8026
www.toadmail.com/~jerispressart/

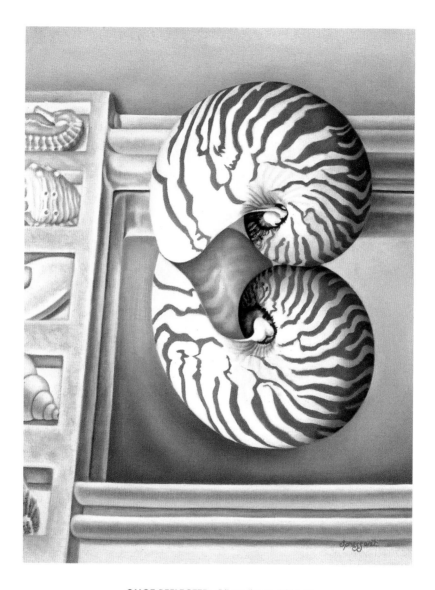

ONCE REFLECTED. Oil on linen. 12" x 9"

"The nautilus shell on the mirror became an exploration of light and color, and a reflection of thought about why expressing myself through the creative process brings joy. I chose the nautilus reflected in the mirror because I kept thinking how much it reminded me of the hemispheres of the brain. Reflection in so many ways." Venues: Silver Bonsai Gallery, Main St. Gallery, Maryland Art Place.

PAPER GRAFT, GRAFT SERIES. Acrylic mixed media on paper. 30" x 19"

"Painting in a series can come from a restriction of format or medium or it can come from the idea that is being explored. I enjoy finding my path with a group of paintings, making them reflect and compound each other. Working abstractly lets me eliminate the visual information until I am satisfied with the composition and structure of the work."
Venues: City Art Studio Gallery, Oerth Gallery, Tutto Bene Gallery.

COMPOSED. Mixed media on watercolor paper. 30" x 22"

"My paintings are composed using the lyrics of our natural surroundings. The power of paint allows the ordinary to become extraordinary." Venues: Louisa Melrose Gallery, Jennings Gallery, Tideline Gallery.

Peter B. Steele

Lafayette, CO • 303.870.1819
www.steelephoto.com

ETHEREAL GATES. Traditional film photography. 20" x 30"

"Crepuscular sun rays accentuated by the humidity in the air backlight these wooden gates guarding field access to an estate in Bedford, NY. This image was captured with my Nikon FM2. I practice traditional film photography, no digital equipment or computer manipulation." Venues: Boulder Open Studios, East Boulder County Artists (EBCA).

Monika Steiner

Fairfax, CA • 707.548.4526
www.monikasteiner.net

BLUE SHADOWS. Oil on wood. 84" x 60"

"My paintings are journals of my emotional life. The creative process centers on the careful balance of color, composition, texture, and mood. I use my inner resonance to capture the essence of an ordinary object, a moment in time, or a memory." Venue: Geras-Tousignant Gallery.

Thalia Stratton

San Francisco, CA • 415.971.5521
www.thaliastratton.com

RED BISTRO. Pastel. 11" x 14"

"I describe my work as a 'visual diary' which focuses on the aesthetic sensibilities dominating classical fine art. The soft, romantic pastels are a passionate reflection of my view. Having journeyed to the culinary meccas of Europe, I executed a body of work reflecting the excitement of European cafe society. The culinary world offers a visual forum to depict one of the most enjoyable aspects of the aesthetic ideal." Venues: Aspect Gallery, Bacchus and Venus, Cornucopia.

Sherri Sugarman

Sausalito, CA • 415.388.9765
cssugarman@comcast.net

SALT WATER TAFFIES. Oil on canvas. 30" x 40"

"I work in oils and would describe my art as 'contemporary realism.' I work from still life and my own photographs. I create color changes and often exaggerate color, form, and shadows. At times I enlarge the images, which allows me to explore abstract qualities found in nature."

Ja Ki Sungail

Felton, CA • 831.335.1734
www.aspenleafstudios.com

ENERGY BARS IN NATURE. Foil on paper. 39" x 28"

"I paint the interaction of energy fields in, around, and through everything at all time. My task is to make visible the invisible and to unite all in a harmonic sea of interaction. I blend biomorphic shapes with industrial forms to create fields of energy."

Carol Surface

Venice, CA • 310.392.9294
cpsstudio@gmail.com

RAVAGED WAYS NO. 25. Mixed media on canvas. 72" x 48"

"This painting is one in a series in which I liken the layers of the human condition to the tearing down and re-generation of the urban landscape. In sidewalks, billboards, and anonymous postings, I see a snapshot of the range of human response...the desperations and fears in communication, the striving for a balance of outstanding passion and centeredness."
Venues: 626 Gallery, Venice Art Walk Annual Studio Tour.

Cat Tesla

Snellville, GA • 770.715.3573
www.artbycat.com

ELEMENTS. Mixed media on birch. 30" x 30"

"Inspired by nature, I select images for my paintings which serve as archetypes of life experiences: a path, a tree, the horizon. My education is in science and graphic design. I think this is why I am compelled to divide a painting into sections of images, color, and texture."
Venue: Lagerquist Gallery.

Diane Tesler

Alexandria, VA • 703.836.6025
www.dianetesler.com

INTERNATIONAL WINTER. Oil on linen. 48" x 60"

"The power of light to reveal form and the beauty of the discarded have been central to my work. Painting is a way to construct a world where opposing forces—light and shadow, order and disintegration, what is lost and what remains—are held in eternal balance." Venues: Torpedo Factory Art Center, Capital Gallery, Midwest Museum of American Art, Sycamore Fine Arts.

Perry Thompson

Cape Coral, FL • 239.772.5408
www.perrythompsonart.com

LONG LIVE THE QUEENS. Film emulsion, oil, pastels, pencil. 19" x 19"

"My paintings are of nature and life, capturing the beauty of all things interacting with each other. I describe my work as *Tempism*—time infused with color and energy." Venues: Tower Gallery, Amsterdam Whitney Gallery.

Helga Thomson

Bethesda, MD • 301.365.8947
www.helgaart.com

SECURITY CHECK. Mixed media on paper. 21" x 30"

"Security Check is part of a series *Here's Looking at You...* Under the gaze of technology our identities become information data creating a dilemma between the intimacy and its violation in the name of unknown otherness." Venue: Gallery Neptune.

Gary V. Trujillo

Denver, CO • 303.743.0424
gtart7@msn.com

PARADISE. Acrylic. 44" x 34"

"Heavily influenced by the French Impressionists, my work explores bas relief use of acrylic media in a series of paintings celebrating Mother Earth and the ancient civilizations she spawned. My style is a playful expression of color and form mixing fantasy and realistic natural depictions in a three-dimensional format."

Ann Curran Turner

Sausalito, CA
415.435.3487

FORBIDDEN FRUIT. Oil on canvas. 36" x 24"

"I see my work as a continuing celebration and exploration of the infinite variety and complexity of human beings on our shared journey. I am driven to capture their elegance, humor, fragility, absurdity—the common vulnerability of our skin, guts, hearts—but most importantly—their attitude, spirit, energy, and life force."

Alan Vaughn

Atlanta, GA • 404.239.0308
alanvaughn@mindspring.com

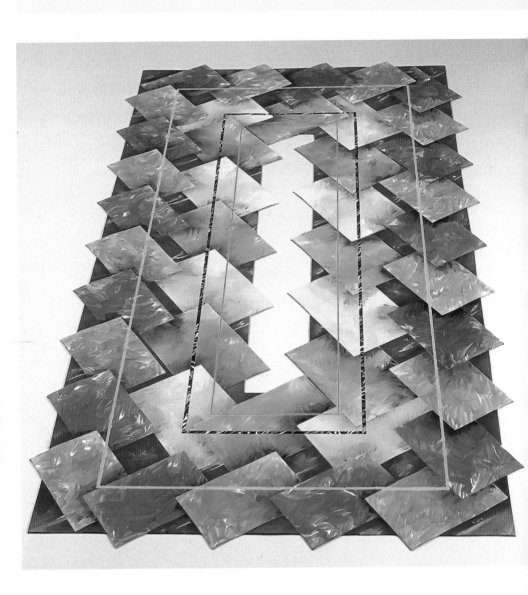

ANTI-RUG. Floorcloth. Varnished acrylic on canvas. 72" x 36"

"My floorcloth creations feature contemporary designs and materials based on a centuries-old tradition blending practicality and beauty. As with any good painting, I want the viewer to discover a new detail each time she sees the piece."

Ran Webber

Buffalo, NY • 716.885.5835
www.ranwebber.artspan.com

MICHAEL. Casein on paper. 48" x 37"

"My work is more about the personal ritual of creating artifact and painted surface than about image making. The finished paintings seem evocative of geometric, figurative sculpture of ambiguous scale, standing within an ambiguous universe." Venues: AbrightKnox Rental Gallery, Florence Biennale.

Idell Weiss

San Francisco, CA • 415.564.2595
www.idellweiss.com

CELEBRATION. Acrylic on watercolor paper. 13" x 19.5"

"Drawing on strong past preference, I began with cool colors, no specific composition in mind, and some untouched open or light areas and some darks to emphasize these. Again, from past experience, I selected the complement of the greens and added some reds and pinks and, lastly, brushed on some overlay of colors to add a feeling of depth." Venues: Aurora Colors Gallery, Hunters Point Spring and Fall Open Studio.

Rod Whyte

Candler, NC • 828.670.8140
www.whytegraphics.com

GHOST OF MOULTRIE. Digital painting on photo paper. 24" x 18"

"The art I create is an extension of the spiritual essence and mysticism I feel from the people and environment around me. Everywhere I look, I see the vibrations and movement of patterns, texture, and color. I then begin, striving for an art which I hope becomes a harmonious whole."
Venues: The Basement Gallery, Three Flights Up.

Stephanie Willis

Portland, OR • 503.977.0985
www.stephaniewillisstudio.com

EXCAVATION. Collage, acrylic on canvas. 40" x 30"

"My mixed media paintings are abstract fields of intense color or earth tones that suggest landscapes or cityscapes. *Excavation* combines elements of collage with multiple layers of textured acrylics. The intricate surface is similar to an archaeological dig, whereby scraping and peeling back each layer reveals clues to previous lives." Venue: Freed Gallery.

SIBLING SUITE. Reduction linocut. 25.5" x 36.5"

"As a kid on vacation, I would spend hours in the pool—always under the water. These are powerful memories: pruney fingers, finding a perfect shell, chlorine-tired eyes, wet swimsuits, warm beach blankets, and the smell of suntan lotion. It is the feeling of these memories I am trying to capture in my work."

Robert Kent Wilson

Washington, DC • 202.288.6934
www.robertkentwilson.com

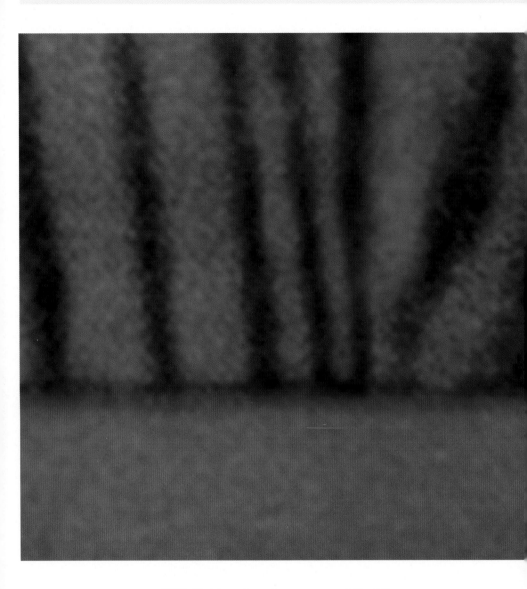

FIELD #9. Ink and acrylic on canvas. 36" x 36"

"This piece is from a series of work that explores striking, abstract landscapes and color fields contrasted by organic patterns and textures. My process is experimental—mixing media that challenge and expand the boundaries of contemporary art."

Marya Wintroub

Sausalito, CA • 415.254.2840
mawint@comcast.net

DARWIN'S THRONE. Graphite on paper. 20.5" x 15"

"I am fascinated by nature and the human condition—real and rendered. In combining representations of both, a narrative is suggested. Inspired by the intimacy between animals and persons still possible in the Galapagos, I've attempted to draw a connection between the islands' ancient creatures and our own human nature and needs." Venues: Industrial Center Building Winter Show, Marin Open Studios.

Marsha Wooley

Centennial, CO • 303.514.5296
www.marshawooley.com

BALANCING ROCK. Oil on canvas. 60" x 96'

"This image extracts the essence and power from an unusual and dramatic rock formation I painted at the Canyonlands of Utah. In *Balancing Rock*, the ponderous weight of a massive, top-heavy rock formation is palpable. This myriad of visual, physical, and emotional sensations is brought to every painting that I create, with an unremitting passion for life itself." Venues: Robischon Gallery, Colorado Gallery of the Arts.

Karyn Young

Fairfax, CA • 415.454.0389
karynyoung@sbcglobal.net

WINE MELODY. Mixed media and collage. 36" x 24"

"This composition extends my examination of the unknown secrets held by the familiar and the challenge to infuse still life with breath and spirit. I strive to provide a balance of recognizing common objects, yet expressing them in a new, quirky, and whimsical light with their own identity. The source comes from an observation and response to my every day life with a random but rhythmic touch that renders the images kinetic."

Ana Zanic

Austin, TX • 512.934.2077
www.anazanic.com

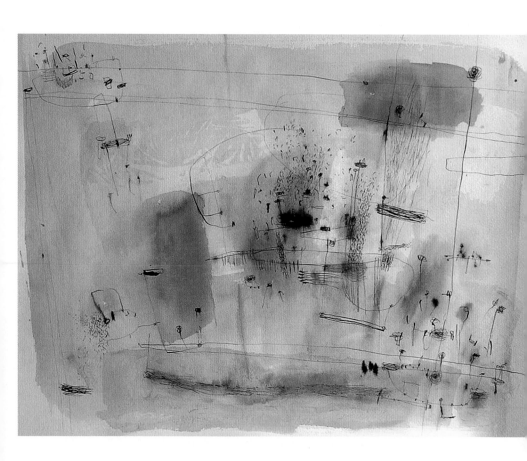

SMALL WORLDS #2. Watercolor, ink on paper. 18" x 24"

"This work belongs to the series of watercolors dealing with the intangibility, elusiveness, and boundlessness of the Universe we live in. Though the unknown confuses and frightens us, at the same time it fills us with curiosity and wonder. Lyrical abstraction, for me, is a path that enables me to express the wondrous and indefinable. This work is currently on display at the Austin City Hall." Venue: Art + Artisans Consulting, Inc.

Carolyn Zaroff

Sausalito, CA • 415.331.9936
www.art.net/czaroff

PURPLE AND GOLD NAPA. Oil on canvas. 16" x 20"

"It was the middle of September, not quite harvest time, approaching late afternoon. The light was intense and the shadows brilliant with deep color. I thought of a dramatic march in the mode of Tchaikovsky, percussive and lyrical. This is what I love most about painting outdoors."

Sheryl Baker

Asheville, NC • 828.273.6995
claygods@hotmail.com

THE HIEROPHANT. Clay, glazes. 25" x 7" x 8"

"My work involves the interpretation of archetypal images. I am particularly interested in the role of animals in dreams and myths, and in our tendency to describe humans using animal characteristics in our effort to understand important events and strong emotions."

Carolyn Barth

Chicago, IL • 773.255.8584
cbwrites@mindspring.com

HEAD. Terra cotta clay. 10" x 6" x 6"

"Sculpting for me is play. Inspired by African, Asian, and primitive masks, I wield a knife and carve planes into clay. As the light dances across the planes, a face emerges, leaving what's meant to be."

JoAnne Bedient

Ft. Myers, FL • 239.482.6754
www.jbedient.com

PIPPI'S TEA POT. Raku-fired ceramic. 11" x 8"

"Bold, contrasting color, drama, whimsy, and graceful forms drive my work. I work in series and enjoy being playful with the subjects I choose. All are hand-built, raku-fired clay."
Venues: Tower Gallery, Raiford Gallery, River Gallery.

BIG KNOB TEAPOT. Earthenware. 10" x 6" x 7"

"Making teapots is the most difficult thing I do as a potter. There are four parts to form and assemble. The proportions and negative spaces all must be right and work together to make a successful piece. Then texture, color, and firings must be right to complete the process."

Lucia R. Briggs

Oakland, CA • 510.277.2375
luciabriggs@earthlink.net

VASES. Wheel-thrown porcelain. 3" to 9" h

"I usually have an idea for a finished piece of porcelain when I sit down at the wheel. I look for balance, elegance, and simplicity. My sketchbooks are filled with patterns and organic shapes I have collected. From these, I hand-draw each one-of-a-kind piece." Venues: Berkeley Potters Guild Christmas and Spring Sale, Association of Clay and Glass Artists of California (ACGA).

Mark Chatterley

Williamston, MI • 517.655.4012
www.chatterley.com

FAIRIE CIRCLE 6. Ceramic. 10' x 4' x 4'

"I create large-scale, sculptural ceramic pieces, focused primarily on the figure, with a metaphysical theme. Surfaces range from a shiny metallic to a crusty texture reminiscent of rusted metal or weathered stone. Work can be placed indoors or out. Bronze castings are available."

Ginny Conrow

Seattle, WA • 206.324.0734
www.conrowporcelain.com

BLUES BASKET. Crystalline-glazed porcelain. 21" x 16" x 15"

"I throw, stretch, and alter the porcelain, the handle following the form, adding height and scale to the piece. I dye, steam, and bend the reeds, weaving them onto the piece with dyed twine. I spray layers of crystalline glazes to accentuate the curves, shadows, and mood of each piece."

Nuala Creed

Petaluma, CA • 707.789.0807
www.nualacreed.com

SWAN CHILD. Hand-built, multi-fired ceramic. 37" x 12" x 12"

"*Swan Child* was inspired by the Irish myth *The Children of Lir*. The children were turned into swans and banished from Ireland for a thousand years. On their return they had a choice to turn back into humans, but they chose to remain swans. To this day their cries can be heard over Ireland."
Venues: Quicksilver Mine Co., Buckeye Sculpture Park.

A CREATURE OF HABIT. Porcelain with stains and glazes. 9.5" x 6" x 5.5"

"Creatures symbolize facets of our psyche that speak or squawk or sing a boundless, wordless song. They are the guardians of hope and the essence of dreams. Like the two sides of every coin, the imagined world and the physical world, they share a common center."

HALO-OPAL PEAR. Raku. 21" x 10"

"Change and growth are important aspects of my work. It should be fun to make pots—playfulness is the key to releasing creative potential. Some of my current work also features melting stained glass on the glaze during the raku firing." Venues: Blue Spiral 1, Carolina Clay Gallery, Carolina Designer Craftsmen, Southern Highland Craft Guild.

Estella Fransbergen

Mount Dora, FL • 352.409.4536
www.estellafransbergen.com

LUCIA. Porcelain. 28" x 16" x 12"

"I design pieces that reflect beauty and natural inspiration. I use my hands to mold each piece while deriving inspiration from nature and my inner need to replace in nature what is being lost. To me, the art speaks of new life and the cultivation of awareness for the mind, body and spirit."

Jane B. Grimm

San Francisco, CA • 415.922.2823
www.janebgrimm.com

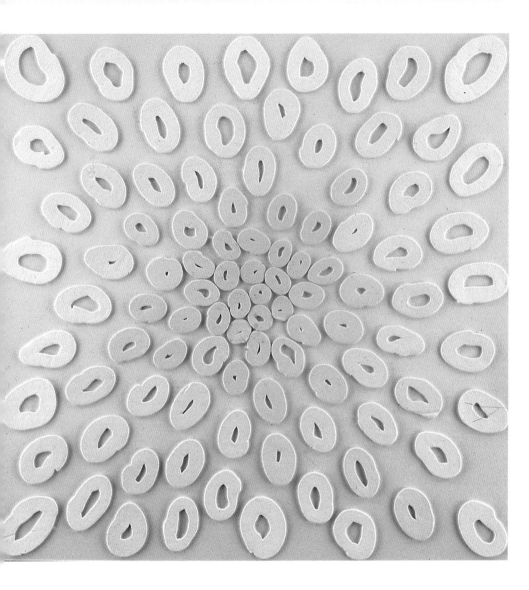

COELENTERATA XIII. Ceramic on wood. 24" x 24" x 2"

"My recent hand-built ceramic sculptures are based upon images seen in nature, plants, sea life, and cells. I use repetition of form, gradation in size, and variation in color to give flow, rhythm, and movement to my work." Venues: Amsterdam Whitney Fine Art, ARTworkSF, Terra Gallery.

Xuan My Ho

Woodside, CA • 650.868.5937
www.swanmosaic.com

COME TO ME! Ceramic, glass, beads, precious stones, coral, stone chips. 36" x 26"

"This eager young woman stands in a torrential rain, desperate and surrounded by obstacles and uncertainty. She reaches passionately for the bird, to persuade it to transform her hopes and dreams into reality." Venues: Kings Mountain Art Fair, Shidoni Gallery.

Judy Hummell

San Francisco, CA • 415.386.0627
jhummell9@aol.com

FIREMARKS. Coiled, burnished, and pit fired clay. 3.5" x 5"

"Drawing inspiration from ancient and primitive pottery, I use methods of the earliest potters
for forming and firing clay. The microcosmic patterns of color are created on my pots by
chance and reflect their singular journey through the elements: earth and water, wind and fire."
Venue: The Highlight Gallery.

Rebecca Koop

Kansas City, MO • 816.483.6964
beckykoop@aol.com

TEA HOUSE WITH BIRD. Extruded stoneware. 6" x 7" x 3"

"I enjoy creating everyday art for my customers' table, kitchen, or home. The *Tea House With Bird* series was created for its sculptural and architectural form, ability to store tea bags, and the ritual of brewing and serving tea." Venues: The Pi Gallery, Phoenix Herb Company, Cokesbury Bookstore.

FLAME WINDOW SCULPTURE. Clay, stained glass, metal stand. 24" x 19.5"

"My art encompasses clay and glass. The clay is smoke-fired to evoke a stone-like finish. The glass allows the light to create its own fire, changing as the light of day changes. This combination of earth and fire uses mandala patterns of old. My aim is to bring the motifs of ancient cultures into a contemporary form." Venues: Secrets, ACC Baltimore.

San Rafael, CA • 415.507.9909
www.drinsomnia.com

HOLY COW. Ceramic, glazes, gold leaf. 33" x 23" x 17"

"The contrast between sacred cows wandering the streets of India and the appalling cattle lot on Route 5 going to L.A. fascinates me. As a first-world country, shouldn't we lead the way in the humane treatment of animals? *Holy Cow* is inspired by the Indian kitsch paintings of Nandi, Vishnu's mount. The hummingbird symbolizes the fragility of life. Her sweater, a rich grass green, is a kinder, more fitting environment." Venues: John Natsoulas Gallery, ACGA Palo Alto Show.

Jeff Margolin

Emeryville, CA • 510.658.8638
http://jeffmargolin.deviantart.com

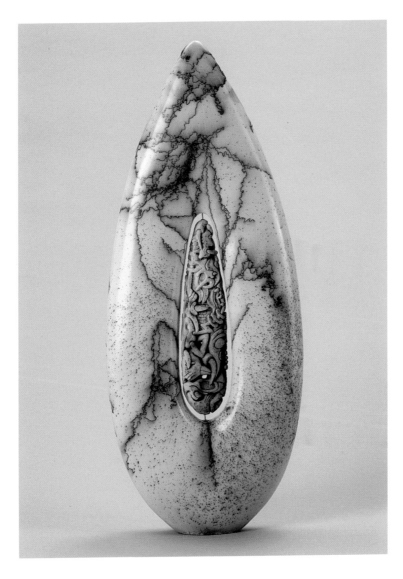

ARROWHEAD. Ceramic. 42" x 15" x 6"

"My work in ceramics has been a process of identifying techniques I favor. The approach I have developed for throwing, carving, burnishing, and form all contain traditional origins. I have combined these elements to create a personal style." Venues: Bella Vetri Gallery, El Prado Gallery.

Jennifer McCurdy

Vineyard Haven, MA • 508.693.0533
www.jennifermccurdy.com

VORTEX VESSEL. Porcelain. 11" x 8" x 8"

"I use a high-fire, translucent porcelain because it can convey qualities of light and shadow I wish to express. I throw my vessel on the potter's wheel, alter the form to set up a movement of soft shadow, then carve patterns to add energy and counterpoint. I fire to cone ten."
Venues: Shaw Cramer Gallery, iota Gallery, Royal Cameo Glass Gallery,

Paddy McNeely

Seattle, WA • 206.723.5153
www.paddymcneely.com

BLACK BAMBOO LANTERN. Ceramic. 13" x 11"

"Inspiration for the lantern is a result of life in the Pacific Northwest. The piece is a fusion of contemporary American and ancient Asian ceramics influences. The clay body is porcelain, wheel-thrown in three pieces, with a cutout pattern. It is fired to 2400 degrees with a heavy reduction atmosphere in a gas kiln. My work is functional, glazed in matte black." Venues: Northwest Craft Center, San Francisco Museum of Craft & Design, Seattle Center Museum of Contemporary Craft.

ARYBALLOID VASE. Ceramic. 30" x 21"

"I owe my life as a potter to the examples set by my teachers, Ishikawa Seiho and Inoue Manji. My work in high temperature terra cotta and porcelain has sought to capture what they sought...the elemental nature of clay and the classic beauty it can convey." Venues: Smithsonian American Art Museum, Peabody Essex Museum, Boston Museum of Fine Arts.

Kathy Pallie

San Rafael, CA • 415.485.5764
kpallie@comcast.net

VESSEL WITH BAMBOO. Ceramic. 26" x 14"

"Strength, beauty, and energy found in my natural surroundings are often the inspiration for my ceramic sculptures. My work is mostly hand-built, allowing me to manipulate the clay to create different forms and surface textures." Venue: Marin Society of Artists.

Greg C. Riley

San Clemente, CA • 949.492.1381
gcrceramic@msn.com

UND. Wheel-thrown lidded vessel with slab construction. 16.5" x 12"

"This collection of work is multi-fired to develop a rich surface blend of colors. Each of these vessels is fired three to four times to reach the desired finish. A wholesale catalog is available upon request."

Jan Schachter

Portola Valley, CA • 650.851.3754
www.janschachter.com

PLATTER. Stoneware with wood ash glaze. 16" x 12.5" x 2"

"I regard making vessels for dining an important aspect of my work. This platter is the perfect vehicle for an elegant presentation of food, whether a modest meal or a formal banquet."
Venues: Snyderman/Works Gallery, Dayle Dunn Gallery, Palo Alto Clay & Glass Festival.

Jean Smith

Denver, CO • 303.377.3945
www.artistregister.com/jeansmith.htm

ALICE IN WONDERLAND SERIES. Tiled plaques. 22" x 27"

"I have been working with clay as my main medium since 1990. This wall piece is part of a series of tiled plaques depicting the twelve chapters of the book *Alice in the Wonderland*. The idea of depicting the chapters of a story appealed to me because I like to work in themes and this gave me a familiar theme to expand upon. It has been a challenging and interesting project." Venues: Core New Art Space, Zip 37 Gallery.

Justin Teilhet

Yellow Springs, OH
937.767.7083

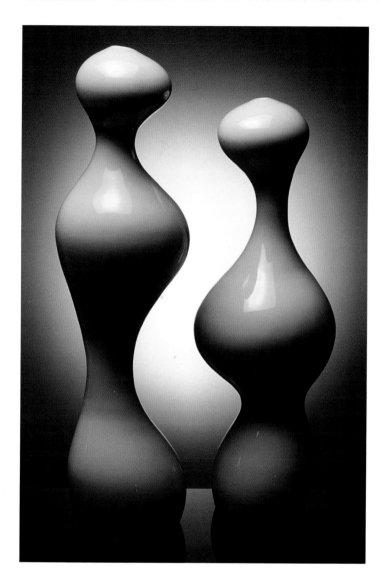

TWO OF US. Porcelain. 24" x 12"

"In many ways my current body of work attempts to capture the visual qualities of liquid. Using the elastic properties of porcelain, I am able to mimic the effects of movement and gravity on a fluid substance. This work is all about surface tension. The pieces are created and displayed in compositions of two or more objects. The interplay and negative space is as important as the objects themselves."

Brenda Townsend

Alexandria, VA • 703.836.2585
www.ceramicappeal.com

KANNON SHRINE BOX. Raku. 12" x 6" x 3"

"The image is a hand-built ceramic box made of slab and coil construction. The inspiration for the boxes come from Japanese and Chinese architecture and garden entries. The box is raku-fired with a hand-made glaze recipe and clear-coated with enamel for years of protection."

Carol Wedemeyer

San Francisco, CA • 415.216.5380
www.carolwedemeyer.org

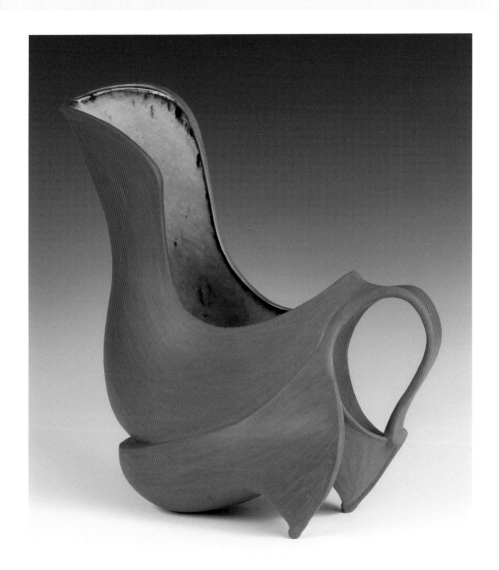

WARTHOG PITCHER. Navajo red clay. 28" x 18" x 12"

"These clay creations, made by using a variety of hand-building techniques, bring together architectural structure and organic form. Often, they are vessels with a figurative or creature reference. This one was inspired by seeing a warthog at the Honolulu Zoo."

Greg Williams

San Anselmo, CA
415.457.5434

LAMP. Porcelain. 16" x 9"

"I have a fascination with illuminating color. In this photo, one of my layered glazes has refracted the light, allowing only the top of the lamp shade to be translucent. Another ceramic surprise."
Venue: Open Studios on the first weekend of December.

Mardi Wood

Bolinas, CA • 415.868.0383
mardiw7@earthlink.net

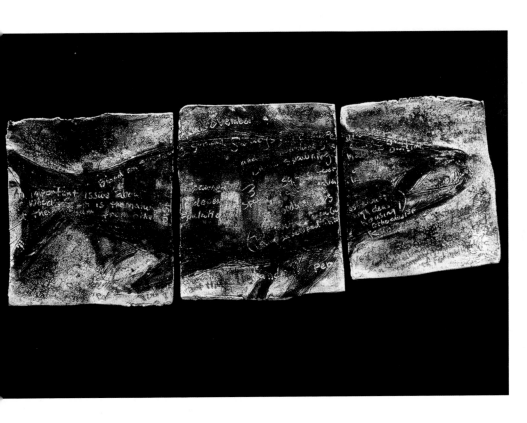

COLUMBIA RIVER CHUM SALMON. Ceramic. 15" x 44"

"This piece combines two media, clay and drawing. Using slabs of clay over which is slathered a porcelain slip, I made an image using dry, powdery mineral oxides. Written into the image is a story of an endangered chum salmon spawning site. Using porcelain, I also make cups and bowls in which I often draw or paint with layers of glaze and ceramic mineral sticks." Venues: Museum of Contemporary Craft, Museum of Craft and Folk Art, ACGA Palo Alto.

David J. Zdrazil

davezdrazil@yahoo.com
www.davezdrazil.com

CAPITAL BUILDING. Wood-fired, wheel-thrown stoneware. 10" x 10" x 10"

"Iconic shapes and forms from my environment are referenced in an abstract way. My intention is to spark a dialogue or idea concerning the condition or importance of these objects I reference, hence, the *Capital Building*."

Lauren Cummings

Airville, PA
717.862.1191

AQUA TORSO. Blown glass. 12" x 8"

"Glass is a challenging medium for expression. Translation from idea to drawing to glass piece is usually a pleasant surprise."

Barbara Allen Dillon

Big Sky, MT • 406.995.2415
www.badillonartglass.com

LADY CHATTERLEY'S BOOKCLUB. Flameworked glass, clay. 14" x 14" x 8"

"This imaginary theme scene is one of three in a series of 'slices of past lives.' The stage is created with hand-built clay furniture with flame-worked glass figures as bookclub members."

FACETED FLORAL PERFUME BOTTLE. Hand-blown glass. 4" x 3"

"Early in my career I decided to put the bulk of my artistic efforts into making perfume bottles. I try to make my designs timeless, unmarred by passing trends, with flavors from the age of excellence, encased in a contemporary form."

Cheryl Hall

Alameda, CA • 510.585.5567
cherylsartwork@yahoo.com

EVOLUTION. Cast glass. 21" x 17" x 8"

"The deep red center of the body radiates the heat of life spreading outward. Living in a world of constantly changing space, darkness and light not separated but moving because the other fills the void. Much of my work investigates the possibility of other realms. I sculpt fire and cast glass, hardwood and metal add tactile quality to the work." Venue: Amsterdam Whitney Fine Art.

Christian Luginger

Amarillo, TX • 806.353.8622
www.flame-one.com

SPRING DANCE. Glass. 12" x 7.5"

"This piece, *Spring Dance*, is one of my first sculptural goblets that inspired me while I was living and studying glass in Venice. Expressing myself with glass is both therapeutic and fascinating." Venues: Vetro Art Glass, Kitrell/Riffkind, National Liberty Museum.

BARRIER REEF PAPERWEIGHT. Encased glass. 3.75" d

"Lundberg Studios was founded by the late James Lundberg. Daniel Salazar has been our resident crystal encasement artist for almost thirty years. His natural designs reflect his love of the ocean and nature. He hopes to inspire good stewardship of our planet." Venues: The New York International Gift Fair, The Buyers Market of American Craft, Metropolitan Museum of Art.

Kari Minnick

Silver Spring, MD • 240.678.8649
www.kariminnick.com

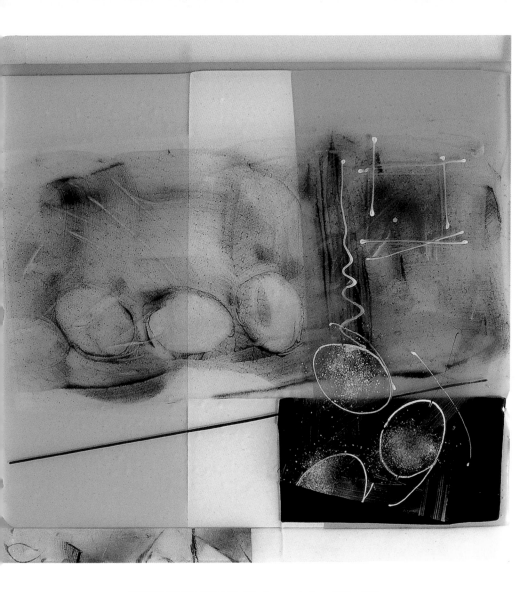

WHICH CAME FIRST #2. Kiln-formed glass. 20" x 20"

"My work explores line, language, and mark making, a fascination for graphic design, and the power of placement. This dialogue in glass delves into the impact of handwritten text, symbols, and their connotations. Eggs may symbolize many things—fragility, strength, vulnerability, and hope, or simply a challenging form to draw." Venue: Morgan Contemporary Glass Gallery.

Damian Priour

Austin, TX • 512.264.2008
www.thechairproject.net

MINIATURE CHAIR. Glass, limestone. 7"

"I have created one hundred miniature chairs made from glass and limestone, each one unique. These chairs will be mailed to about one hundred artists who will be asked to, in return, create a chair of their own making. The idea behind *The Chair Project* stems from a long tradition of artists trading with artists."

Matt Seasholtz

Johnson, VT • 802.635.2731
www.windsedgestudio.com

RAINBOW BOTTLE. Blown glass. 16" x 12" x 3"

"I am fascinated by the fluid nature and optical properties of glass. I begin each piece with multiple overlays of colorful transparent glass and create surface texture using an optic mold. The final organic forms explore the interplay between color, form, and light."
Venues: ACC Shows, Art Resources Gallery, Idyllwild Gallery.

Terrie Barns-Canfield

Des Moines, WA • 253.839.0887
tjbcdesign@aol.com

THE GIFT. Neckpiece. Sterling silver, Tahitian pearls, freshwater pearls. 26" x 16" x 2"

"Moon reflecting on water, sea grasses caressing rock, bamboo whispering in wind...nature's dynamic forces inspire my jewelry. Interweaving textured, contoured fine metals and gem stones, create sculptural expressions of the natural world that touch the interior landscape of the wearer.' Venues: ACC Shows, Shidoni Galleries and Sculpture Gardens, Objects of Desire Gallery.

Sana Doumet

Clearwater, FL • 727.455.5802
www.sanadoumet.com

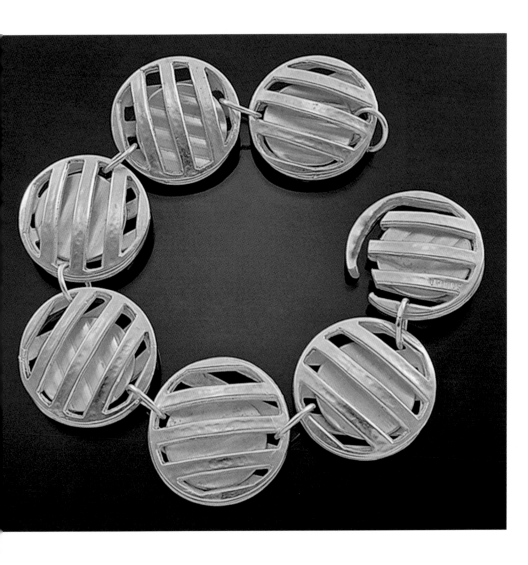

PICKA BOO. Bi-metal (22k gold and sterling silver), sterling silver. 7.5"

"Different cultures and countries I have lived in are the source of my inspiration. The combination of gold and silver create a contrast in the jewelry. The various shapes, lines, textures—and vivid use of the hammer—give softness to the metal, allowing the jewelry to be both smooth and fun to the touch." Venues: ACC Sarasota, Winter Park Sidewalk Art Festival, Boca Raton Museum Art Festival.

Joy Fonvielle

New Braunfels, TX • 830.625.5664
silicadreams@earthlink.net

PLANET SWIRL. Effetre glass from Italy, sterling wire, sterling beads. 2" x 3"

"The movement of wire makes this such a unique piece. The swan clasp echoes the movement of the wire." Venues: Wimberley Glass Works, New Braunfels Art League.

Debra Lynn Gold

Atlanta, GA • 404.239.0308
debralynngold@mindspring.com

STACKED. Earrings. Sterling silver, colored aluminum. 1.75"

"I place playful elements within formal, engineered spatial structures. The playfulness comes as parts rotate, interlock, slide, spin, flex, or flip. I believe that jewelry should be as dynamic as the human form on which it is worn. It should distinguish itself as well as the person who has chosen to wear it."

Michael Good

Rockport. ME • 207.236.9619
avi@michaelgood.com

RUFFLE CUFF AND TORQUE EARRINGS. Patinated bronze, 22k gold

"My work continues to examine the subtle changes and the consequent visual effects of a plane as it moves non-definitively through space. I do this by continuing my development of the technique of anticlastic raising. It has proven to be the ideal method for generating elemental structures that illustrate and help to explain more complex movements inherent in organic life."

Tom Herman

Stone Ridge, NY • 845.687.2137
www.sevenfingers.com

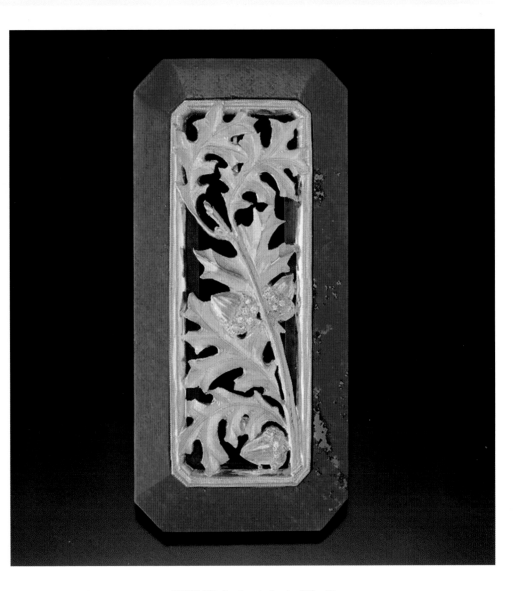

BROOCH. Red oak, lapis. 21" x 1"

"My jewelry is inspired by the natural world—shapes that cannot be improved upon, rhythms so familiar they go unnoticed. After cutting the lapis, I inlay the gold plate and cut the border. I carve red oak leaves and acorns, carve it into the gold, engrave the leaves and acorns, and set the diamonds. A final chasing gives the element of texture and shape, sculpting the gold."
Venues: American Craft Expo, Virginia Museum of Fine Arts, Timeless Treasures Jewelry Fair.

Howard Lazar

West Bloomfield, MI • 248.538.4696
www.hldesigns-inc.com

PENDANT. 14k gold, sugilite, citrine, diamond. 1.2"

"I love to create unusual pieces with an emphasis on wearability. My work is done in casting, in fabrication, and sometimes in both. A variety of unique and colorful gemstones help to electrify the pieces. I look forward to pushing the boundaries of my designs. This pendant has a half circle of sugilite, a 6.15ct pear shape citrine prong set, and a .15pt bezel set floating diamond."

Patricia Madeja

West Islip, NY • 631.661.2509
callahanmadeja@earthlink.net

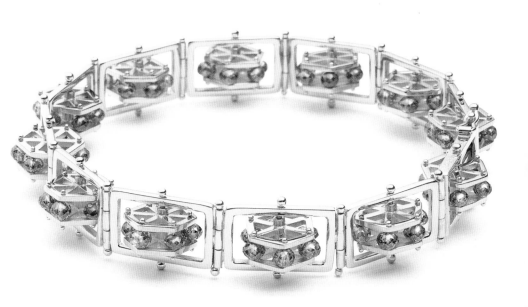

FERRIS WHEEL BRACELET. 18k gold, champagne diamonds. 7.5"

"Geometric forms and elements of architectural structures influence my designs. Movement is an important aspect of each piece and I enjoy the challenge of engineering and fabricating the mechanisms that will enable motion within the work. This unique bracelet spins with playful elegance for the discerning collector to enjoy." Venues: ACC Baltimore, Aaron Faber Gallery, Guild.com.

Valerie Mitchell

Los Angeles, CA • 213.687.3987
www.valeriemitchell.com

TIARA FOR A WALK ON FOURTH STREET BRIDGE. Silver, pearls, flowers. 6" x 5"

"Imagine a walk on the 1930s bridge overlooking the Los Angeles riverbed, picking leaves from wild grapes that once flourished there, and displaying them in a tiara inspired by the tri-leaf portals of the Beaux Arts bridge in my neighborhood." Venues: Craft In America Museum Tour, Portland Museum of Contemporary Craft, Velvet Da Vinci.

Louise Norrell

Athens, GA • 706.549.5306
www.metalhead.biz

TAHITIAN PEARL RING. 18k yellow and white gold, 9mm Tahitian pearl

"My inspiration comes from the lush colors, fabrics, and textures of the tropics and the fragmented appearance of old, falling down buildings. Also, for better or worse, the comics always influence me. Growing up I read every comic strip, *New Yorker* cartoon, and issue of *Mad Magazine* when I should have been doing my homework." Venues: Aurum Studios, Topaz Gallery, Carolina Designer Craftsmen Show.

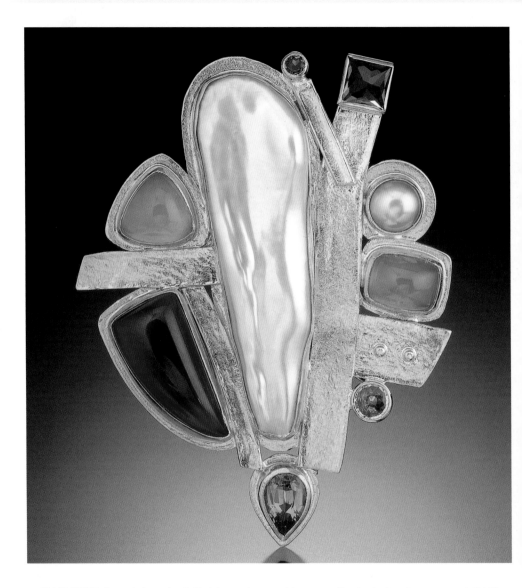

PEARL RIVER. Brooch/pendant. Gold, pearls, sapphires, amethyst, chalcedony, garnet. 2.12"

"This brooch/pendant is roller-printed, hand-formed, constructed, and soldered. Color is important to the work. This I get from hand-picked pearls and gems stones, both precious and semi-precious, in various combinations of balance and composition. I design each fine art jewelry piece with the ability to stand on its own, which attracts the individual collecting, wearing, and enjoying my art."

JacQueline Sanchez

Atlanta, GA • 404.441.5225
www.jacquelinesanchez.com

FOREVER YOUNG RINGS. Sterling silver, sandblasted plastic, diamond, 14k yellow gold

"I approach my work as small sculpture, concerned with line and geometric form to produce bold, expressive statements. Each piece is the result of combining technique with artistic vision." Venues: American Craft Council Shows, Philadelphia Museum of Art Craft Show, Beehive Co-op Gallery.

Marie Scarpa

Petaluma, CA • 707.765.6558
www.mariescarpadesigns.com

BLUE MOON PIN/PENDANT. 18k, platinum, abalone pearl, green tourmaline, sapphires. 2.25"

"My hand-woven jewelry collections are mosaics of creative expression. By applying fiber techniques to gold using the simplicity of primary shapes, these woven sculptures reveal their fluidity and depth as seen in the geometry of nature. These unique pieces evoke dreamcatchers, kaleidoscopes, and contemporary filigree."

Ilene Schwartz

Chester, NY • 845.469.6412
isjdesigns@optonline.net

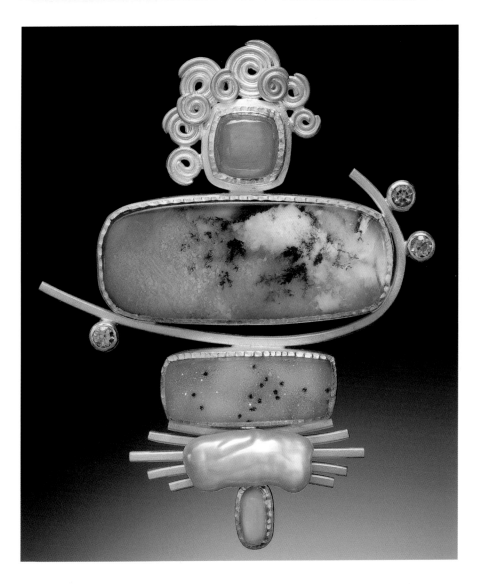

WOMAN IN PURPLE. 18k gold, grossular garnet, amethyst sage, tanzanite, drusy, pearl. 2.5"

"I use high karat gold and a variety of stones with unusual textures and patterns to create classic, feminine forms. By keeping the shapes simple, the contrast of textures and the combination of colors remain the focus of the design." Venues: ACC Baltimore, Langman Gallery, Klay Gallery.

Tobi Sznajderman

Amherst, MA • 413.549.7697
www.tobisznajderman.com

WEDDING SET. 18k gold, diamonds

"I strive to create works that have a rhythm or tell a story. I am intrigued by contrasts—polished edges and the sparkle of a diamond add life to a matte surface."

Wayne Werner

Havre de Grace, MD • 410.942.0027
waynewerner@mindspring.com

MOKUME RINGS. 14k white gold, silver mokume, 18k yellow gold or platinum side rails

"The best compliment I can get is to have someone ask me to make their wedding band.
These rings are made from 14k white gold and silver *mokume*, a Japanese word meaning
eye of the wood. Many layers of metal are fused together, twisted, and forged to produce
a labyrinth of patterns. I invite couples to come into my studio and work on their own bands,
a rewarding experience for all involved."

Judi Wood

West Palm Beach, FL • 561.689.7156
www.judiwood.com

FANDANGO. Glass beads, precious gems, 18k gold, silk lining. 7" x 5" x 2"

"Each design I create is woven bead-to-bead, one bead at a time, and free-hand. I work with glass beads, precious gems, precious metals, and found objects weaving with a needle and monofilament thread. My inspiration is derived from nature, my imagination, and dreams."
Venues: Polk Museum of Art, Orlando Museum of Art, Gasparilla Festival of the Arts.

Debra Adelson

Collingswood, NJ • 856.240.1055
www.funkyflatware.com

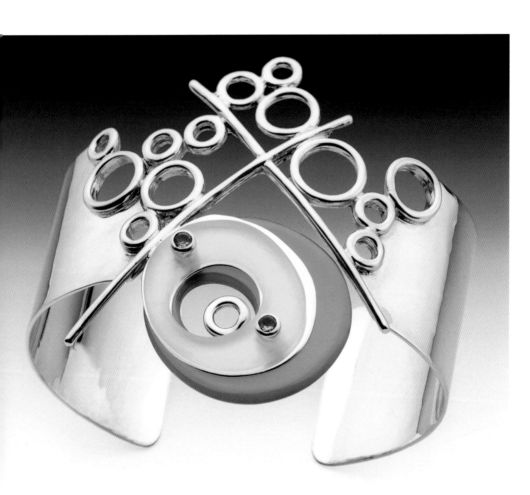

INTERSECTION CUFF BRACELET. Sterling silver, hand-carved acrylic, sky blue topaz. 3" x 2"

"I pride myself on a line of jewelry, Judaica, tableware, and giftware that features a mixture of innovative design and a fashion-forward use of color. All of my work is made from a combination of hand-carved acrylic and hand-fabricated sterling silver." Venue: American Craft Council Shows, Washington Craft Show.

KOL-AMI STAR. Granite and stainless steel on marble. 7.5' x 6.5' x 4'

"The *Kol Ami Star* is from a recent series of outdoor sculptures. It is important in public artwork, to address issues of society and community. Joining individual pieces of different granites around a central identity symbolically coheres our innate sense of contribution and belonging. Like the granite from different parts of the world, we all come from the same piece of real estate. Each of us has the shared value and responsibility to help heal and protect our planet."

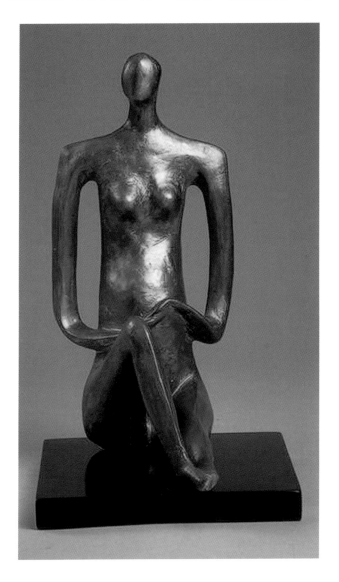

SERENITY. Bronze. 14" x 7" x 12"

"The smooth, flowing lines and upward movement of *Serenity* represent the human soul at peace. The meditative figure is filled with contentment and a quiet spirituality, as it awaits life's endless possibilities." Venue: Infusion Gallery.

Cheryl Barnett

Merced, CA & San Leandro, CA
www.barnettsculpture.com • 209.384.3602

VESSEL OF THE INNOCENTS #III. Cast bronze. 79" x 27" x 12"

"In the medium of cast bronze sculpture, my focus is the human body for its universal identification, complexity, and mystery. I abstract the figure by concentrating on the minimal qualities of line and space through gestural simplicity. My portfolio of work represents people I've known, relationships, experiences, and popular myth." Venue: Eleonore Austerer Gallery.

Julie Booth

Vienna, VA
www.threadborn.com

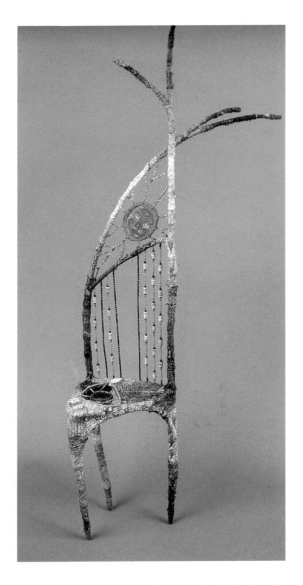

LONGING, CHAIR SERIES. Mixed media. 27" x 6" x 5"

"Chairs reference human anatomy. In my *Chair* series, I play with blurring the line between human characteristics (specifically the human face) and this inanimate object. My recent pieces have become more altar-like, placing the human presence within an environment. I like to think of these pieces as visual poems." Venues: Potomac Craftsmen Fiber Gallery, RiverView Gallery.

SHELL WOMAN. Bronze. 22" x 8.5" x 10"

"Ancient, universal images appear in my dreams. Thus came *Shell Woman*. Egyptian stone figures and Greek goddesses inspired me. *Shell Woman* has an inscription in shell hieroglyphs on the vertical slab behind her. Hand-built in clay, then cast in bronze, with a unique patina on her chambered nautilus body."

Don Carlson

Richmond, CA • 510.410.7833
www.rudedesigns.com

BOBBY-Q. Found objects, welded metal. 6' 4" x 30" x 18"

"My name is *Bobby-Q.* I'm a fully functional barbeque made from recycled material. Let me hold your drink while you baste my ribs and poke at my meat. Smoke vents through my eyes, ears, and mouth like the overweight, chain-smoking alcoholic that I am. Can I use your bathroom?"

Mindy Z. Colton

Orlando, FL • 407.568.7780
www.mindycolton.com

LEAP OF FAITH. Bronze on a granite base. 24" x 15" x 15"

"Many of my works focus on using the horse as a metaphor for the human experience. I hope to create positive energy or elicit a thoughtful feeling or mood. Working in clay and wax I create both one-of-a kind and limited-edition works in bronze, and larger works in aluminum and other media. My sculptures are expressionistic, abstract, figurative, and symbolic."
Venues: Museum of Florida Art, Grand Bohemian Gallery, Artistic Hand Gallery.

James D. W. Cooper

Greensboro, NC • 336.707.9370
www.coopermetals.com

LIBATION. Fountain sculpture. Cast bronze. 116" h

"*Libation* is the sculptural centerpiece for a newly-created park in the center of downtown Greensboro. This piece was designed to serve as the apparent source or spring for a large water feature in the park. Its inspiration came from the phrase 'my cup runneth over,' and the abundant green space in the city."

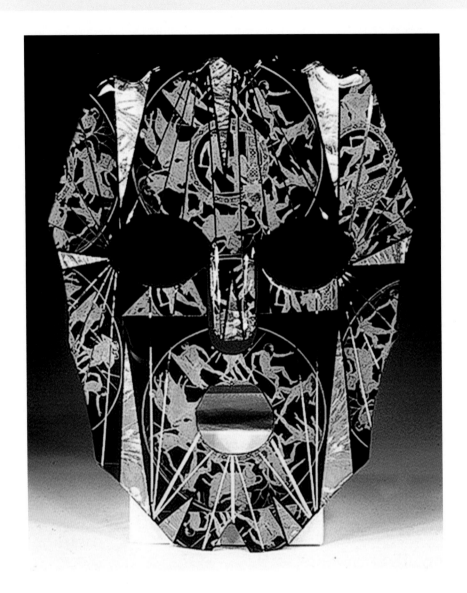

GREEK ANTIQUITIES MASK. Fiberglass, brass. 12" x 10" x 4"

"Using a multi-dimensional graphic arts technique applied to brass metal with fiberglass, I strive to evoke the greatness of our cultural and historical past bringing to the present a reminder of past grandeur. These images of Theseus and the Minotaur come from museum vases six hundred years old. The mask represents what we hide from ourselves during wartime." Venues: Artemis Gallery, Virginia Museum, ACC Shows, Amsterdam Whitney Gallery.

DREAM MACHINE. Recycled tools, toys, and game pieces. 18" x 8" x 6"

"Currently I am fascinated with laboratory devices, gadgets, machines, and futurism.
Elaborating on gears, cams, and screws I create machines that compel people to
play. I find great reward in creating a more elaborate method of accomplishing less."

BIRD IN THE HAND. Cast bronze. 45" x 16"

"*Bird in the Hand* is a sculpture that combines strong, humble, masculine support with a carefree, feminine flight of fancy. It is a story of commitment and part of my ongoing *Duet* series."
Venues: Jones & Terwilliger Galleries, Breckenridge Fine Art Galleries, Galerie du Soleil.

Stephen Fitz-Gerald

Santa Rosa, CA • 707.584.0182
www.sfitzgeraldfineart.com

TOPOGRAPHIC EMOTIONS. Welded steel. Lifesize

"I create sculpture, and design and fabricate functional decorative art from furniture and jewelry to large, site-specific outdoor structures: fountains, gates, gazebos, trellises, and winery doors. Knowledge of historical styles and artifacts allows me to design and build pieces that match aesthetically any period from Neolithic Bronze Age to Industrial Modern."

#154. Welded steel. 14" x 12" x 14"

"My sculptures express the idea that metal can appear to be weightless. I work intuitively, and the various shapes and textures of the metal I use inspire my sculptures. My work challenges the traditional concepts of balance and space."

TEMPEST. Bronze. 36" x 16" x 14"

"In all my work, what I find most fascinating is the creative process itself. My two-dimensional and three-dimensional forms expose the experience of the creation of the artwork. *Tempest* is from the series *Celestial Offerings*. The process of creating the sculptures is kept evident in the ripped and torn textures that lead to lava-like forms. Images of a spirited universe come to mind where spiraling figures dance and lotus flowers emanate."

Guilloume

Sandia Park, NM • 505.286.9710
www.guilloume.com

DREAMS. Bronze relief. 12" x 36"

"I practice *Bolismo*, a self-described, emotion-filled style using modest forms, textures, and shading to portray the vast range of human feelings—from the simple visages of routine daily interactions to those highly complex expressions reflecting the depths and heights of the earthly experience with all its joy, afflictions, hopes, and fears."

Gregory Johnson

Cumming, GA • 770.887.1561
www.gregoryjohnson.biz

GATHERING OF THE MAGNIFICENT. Bronze. 48" x 52" x 47"

"I like to create animated, softly detailed sculptures with expressive features that maintain classical proportions. When I work with wild life as a theme, I enhance their character by adding movement and geometric designs." Venues: Shidoni Sculpture Garden, Loveland Invitational Show on odd years.

Bluffton, SC • 843.757.8450
www.stephenkishel.com

FIRST IMPRESSIONS. Powder-coated aluminum. 72" x 18" x 12"

"We are so much more than meets the eye, so why are we so quick to judge another? If only we could wait until we know a person before we passed judgment and closed up our mind. Then and only then would we know what we don't know, and perhaps see more, learn more and as a result be more." Venues: Editions Limited Gallery of Fine Art, The Gallery at Beaufort, South Carolina Artisans Center.

Darlis C. Lamb

Englewood, CO • 303.779.4527
www.darlislamb.com

FRENCH LESSON 8 - ORANGE EPLUCHÉE AVEC DEUX PRUNES. Bronze. 5.5" x 13" x 11.5"

"I have taken the concept of still lifes as one would think of in a painting and transposed my ideas into bronze. These subjects allow me to focus on beauty, form, and design in the most classic sense. The series is called *French Lessons*, keeping it within a context of continuity."
Venues: Peterson-Cody Gallery, Churchill Gallery, Riverbend Fine Art.

Bruce R. MacDonald

Burlington, VT • 800.639.1868
www.brmdesign.com

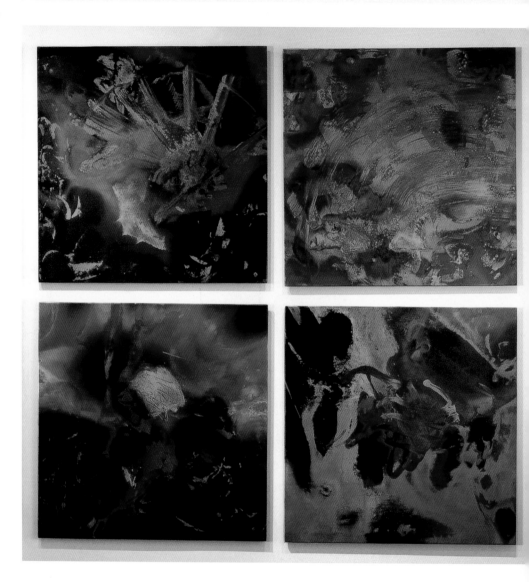

FORCES IN SPACE. Flamed copper. 23" square

"These copper panels have a patina finish developed by chemical reaction and tremendous heat. I developed a technique of painting using super-heated gases, snow, chemical washes, wood blocking, soot water, sand, etc. to generate images from the oxidation formed on the metal surface."

Lisa Slovis Mandel

San Diego, CA • 858.490.1336
www.lisaslovis.com

COUPLING. Salt and pepper shakers. Pewter. 4.5"

"Developed around characteristics of childhood toys, natural beauty, everyday play, and traditional ceremonial objects, these pieces can be used, re-arranged, and played with. Although abstract, they are reminiscent of a couple that fit together, yet have an elegant gap to show that they are one on their own also." Venues: Sausalito Arts Festival, Scottsdale Arts Festival, Birmingham Art Fair.

Thomas R. Markusen

Kendall, NY • 585.659.8001
www.markusenmetal.com

WINDOWS. Collage. Raspberry patina on copper. 36" d

"Strongly influenced by the southwestern landscape, I utilize abstract and simplified shapes in my copper metalwork to create semi-functional objects that reflect the vastness, texture, and dramatic lighting of this environment. I continue to be fascinated by the malleability of copper and its diverse palette of colors." Venues: LeKAE Gallery, Milward Farrell, Austin Presence.

Monty Monty

Santa Rosa, CA • 707.546.6064
www.montymontyart.com

THE KNIGHT RIDER. Assemblage. 29" x 40" x 14"

"Storming the centuries between two disjacent millennia, bringing the valor and gallantry
of the Iron Age to Postmodern Art, this is *The Knight Rider*. Selected relics have been assembled
to form a mounted knight in armor. This recycled scene melds two disparate worlds, the
leaden steel of the Middle Ages with the buzzing, light crush of recycled aluminum."
Venues: The Quicksilver Mine Company, I. Wolk Gallery.

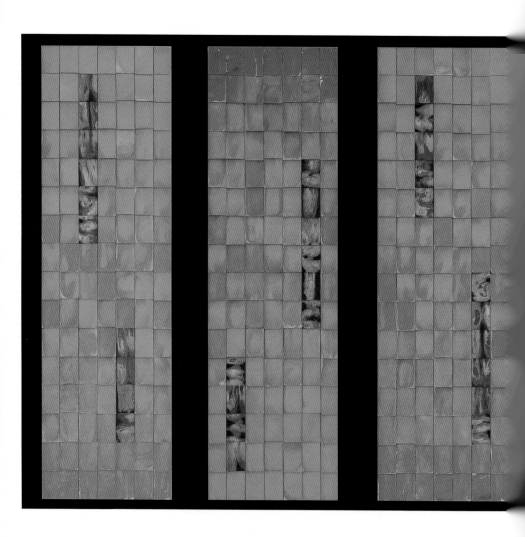

TRIPTYCH. Copper over wood panel. 48" x 15" x 3" each

"We have been creating metal sculptures together since 1998. Our focus is contemporary abstract wall sculpture. We are concerned with rhythm, color, texture, and line all working together to create an object of tranquil, sometimes dynamic, beauty. We thrive on pushing the medium to go beyond craft into sophisticated, expressive artwork." Venues: Pinnacle Gallery, Earthenworks Gallery, Chepita Gallery.

Zak Zaikine

Sebastopol, CA • 707.823.9340
www.zakzaikine.com

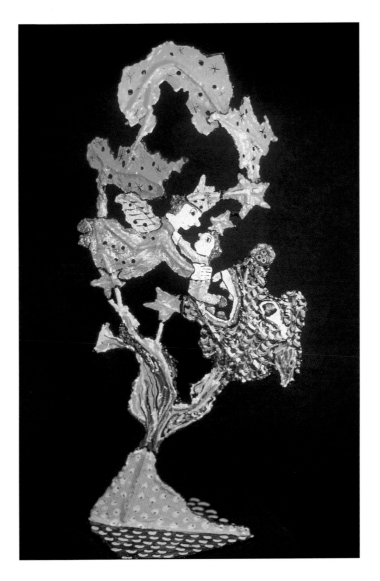

JUST IN TIME. Steel. 22" x 12" x 11"

"Drawing on a deep repertoire of narrative elements, I utilize them in an extremely expressive link between text and imagery, awakening in us our hidden impulses and childhood fantasies. I hope to take the viewer to a journey imaginable only in art." Venue: Bodega Landmark Studio Gallery.

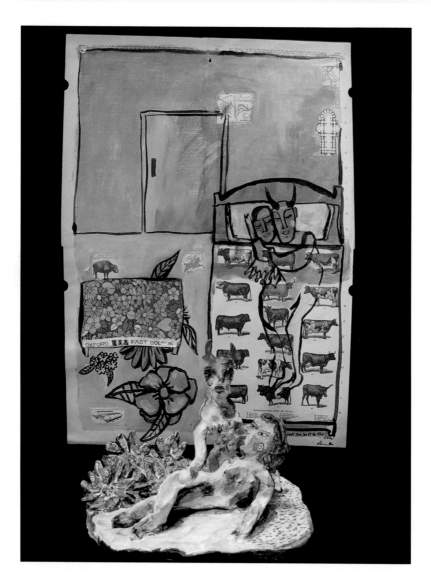

STEER THE BULL TO THE COW. 1914 dictionary, acrylic, fabric, ceramic. 22" x 17"

"My fascination with this project is that it brings language into the realm of visual expression. Being nearly a century old, the dictionary evokes the history that informs language as well as visual art to this day. I interpret imagery from the dictionary paintings in ceramic sculpture to create pairs." Venues: SFMOMA Artists Gallery, The Fine Art Museums of San Francisco.

Frank Colson

Sarasota, FL • 941.321.0129
www.colsonart.com

CIRCUS HORSE SERIES II. Coated bronze, cherrywood base. 64" x 29" x 13"

"As a professional sculptor, the core theme of my work is the 'horse.' I look at this subject
from a multi-faceted point of view unrelated to the animal itself."

TAILWAG TERRIER. Plastics, brass and stainless hardware, exterior housepaint. 15" x 16" x 7"

"Inspired by traditional American whirligigs, our mechanical sculptures are a combination of art and science. We use contemporary plastics, exterior house paint, and metal hardware to re-invent old ideas. Our whirligigs enlarge upon nature and make the wind visible."

Joan Danziger

Washington, DC • 202.686.5285
joansculp@aol.com

ANTLER LADY. Mixed media over wire armature. 28" x 37" x 27"

"The use of animal imagery as metaphorical or psychological subject has great potency to me. It gives my sculptures a life of their own and creates a magical world. My work represents my personal mythology, whose focus is on people's relationship with each other, and to the world around them."

Suzi K. Edwards

Maitland, FL • 407.645.4183
www.suzikedwards.com

YIN/YANG UNDER THE SEA. Porcelain, metallic lustres, sea shells, glass jewels. 11" x 10" x 7"

"*Yin/Yang Under the Sea* is a humorous, romantic fantasy, built upon a hunk of coral I found in St. Thomas eons ago. The figures are sculpted out of porcelain, painted with underglazes, and enhanced with seashells, lustres, and metallics. Most of my work these days is large-scale public art; these small intimate pieces reveal my inner thoughts and desires." Venues: Orlando Shakespeare Theater, Florida Botanical Gardens, Orlando International Airport.

Richard Feese

Sacramento, CA • 916.455.5591
www.richardfeese.com

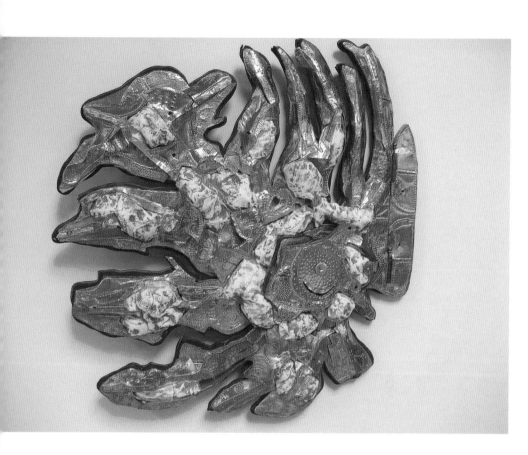

THE FJORDS. Wood, stucco, copper. 47" x 45" x 7"

"Maps have powerful visual stimuli. One can become completely absorbed in the adventure of a mind's dream of a place while looking at a map. What you see here is a map of an area of the fjords in Norway, part of a series of map constructions I have built over the years."
Venue: SFMOMA Artists Gallery, Crocker Art Museum.

Cherie E. Hacker

Sacramento, CA • 916.704.2909
www.asylumgallery.net

LAMP & ENDTABLE ROUNDS. Mixed media. 20" diameter each

"As the *Lamp & Endtable* project develops, it appears to me as a 'domestic icon.' It relates to the American household and family. The lamp, source of intellectual illumination, anchors itself on a generic framework. My aesthetics lean toward mixed media, therefore, I investigate the subject with all possible media." Venues: Asylum Gallery at Headquarters for the Arts, Alliance of Women Artists.

Jane Herrick

Eau Claire, WI • 715.833.9745
herricjl@uwec.edu

OLD MAN RIVER. Mixed media. 25" x 19" x 5"

"My themes deal with the mystery of human presence, using various resources. I use materials to express emotional relationships and life experiences, translating them into life forms or images. This invites the viewer not only to question the meaning of the piece, but also its structure and materials." Venues: Vision Gallery, Foster Art Gallery.

RELIQUARY. Mixed media. 21.5" x 15" x 18.5"

"Looking like mossy bark on the outside, *Reliquary* opens to reveal an unexpected, delicately embroidered and inscribed inside panel. I designed this piece to express my concerns for the environment and used the implied reference to a religious object to emphasize our moral connection to nature."

Kelly Buntin Johnson

Dearborn, MO • 816.450.3616
www.diddy-wa-diddy.com

SUMMIT OF INTERCESSORS. Mixed media. 14" x 24" x 13"

"Beckoned by Nightmarchers (forgotten ancient ones who come out at night) Secretary Lucky Bird distributes pages from the pilgrim's handbook to fellow Knights of Peregrine Intercessors...Lean away so that others may breathe...Walk gently with honor...Re-adjust the sacred compass."

Russell Kimsoc

Boulder, CO • 303.941.2363
www.russellkimsoc.com

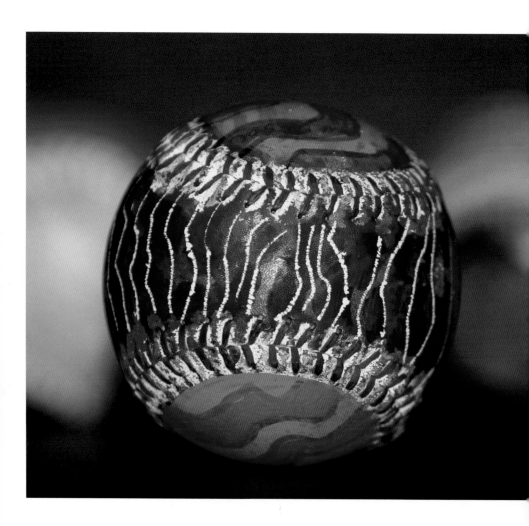

NORTH OF NANKOWEAP. Mixed media on leather. 4" x 4" x 4"

"Painting on a round structure, an orb, provides a strange sense of continuity. These balls are for pure enjoyment and curiosity. They are interactive art and intended for play."

Aaron Kramer

Venice, CA • 310.664.6700
www.urban-objects.com

HALF AND HALF. Wood, wire, foundation washers, stamp ball. 24" x 9"

"In this piece, a welded steel armature is woven over with recycled street sweeper bristles and reclaimed, re-sawn hardwoods. My sculptural work is often woven or constructed. By exploring the intersection between the found and the fabricated. I seek a deeper understanding of the transcendent nature of ordinary objects. A sense of whimsy runs through my work repurposing media. Remember, 'trash' is a failure of the imagination."

ICE WOMAN SCULPTURE GROUP. Clay, glaze, steel armature and stand. 41" x 6"

"My inspiration is from the ancient civilizations of the world, including Mesopotamia and Oceania. I try to give my work a sense of the past, and process is an important element."
Venues: Hammerfriar Gallery, The di Rossa Preserve.

Tomas Savrda

Kent, NY • 860.364.5887
tomassavrdaartcraft@volny.cz

SHOOTING GALLERY. Kinetic object. Recycled metal and wood. 15" x 13"

"Venturing into the fantasy world, I try to create playful or serious ancient-looking kinetic objects using recycled metal and wood, preserving as much as possible the original patina of the material." Venues: Human Arts Gallery, Fire Opal Gallery, Left Bank Gallery.

Roberta Smith

Salida, CO • 719.539.1732
www.robertasmithart.com

CLOTHED ONLY IN KNOWLEDGE THEY SET OUT UPON LIFE'S ADVENTURE. Mixed media. 29" x 36" x 5"

"History, memory, dreams, and the reflexive pursuit of knowledge are vital. Old books and papers bear the patina of their past and possess more stories than the ones imprinted upon them when they were new. To collect venerable discards and endow them with new life and meaning enthralls me."

Thomas Spake

Chattanooga, TN • 423.596.8696
www.thomasspakestudios.com

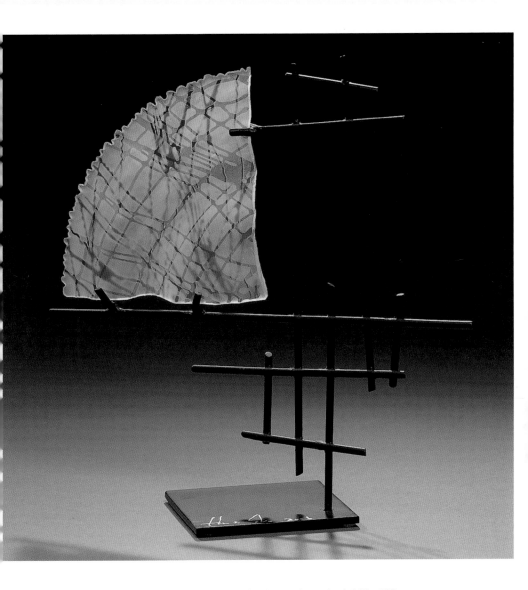

PEPPERMINT, LINEAR SERIES. Blown glass, steel. 15" x 13"

"The *Linear* series combines blown, cut, and etched glass with steel, to create a complete composition. The interest in this series stems from a fascination with the subtleties of architecture and the ebb and flow of infrastructure."

PROSPECTS. Copper, bronze, titanium, stainless steel. 24" x 13"

"My sculptures seek to celebrate the diversity, complexity, and randomness of the world. I combine images and materials from industry, nature and ordinary life. I believe in the power of objects to transcend language and cultural barriers. By combining seemingly disparate elements I create a harmony within the work." Venues: Rosenberg Kaufman Fine Art, www.sculpture.org.

Helen Wilson

Ramona, CA • 760.803.2857
helenwilsonartist@mac.com

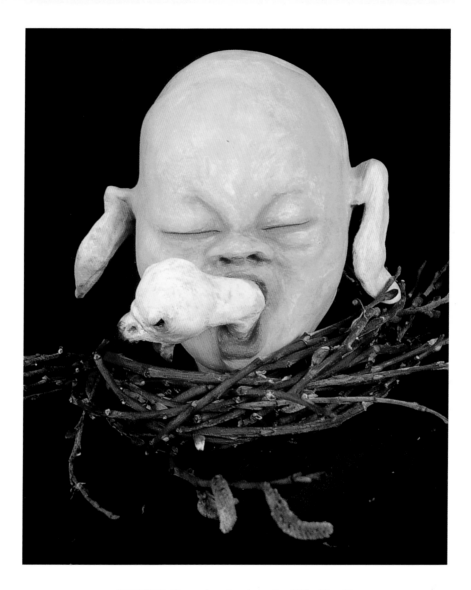

BABYBIRD. Ceramic mixed media. 12" x 8" x 6"

"I am playing with child as myth, child as animal, child as toy. And in that vein a morphing has begun. When we turn a child into a myth, does part of what it 'is' remain? The parts we manage to change, do they change as intended or do whole new evolutions begin somewhere between the intent and reality?" Venues: Santa Ysabel Art Gallery, Eklektikas.

Melissa Woodburn

San Rafael, CA • 415.499.1655
www.melissawoodburn.com

SHADOWS THROUGH THE TREES. Ceramic, pine needles. 16" x 18" x 6"

"This piece is part of my *Undulate Vessel* series, combining ceramic with flowing coils of pine needles. Items in this series each convey a sense of place—in this case a quiet glen in the tall trees. The underglazes and glazes flow over the clay body suggesting deepening layers of shadows, revealing a private sanctuary." Venues: Lucas Valley Open Studios, Marin Open Studios, Marin Society of Artists.

Nancy Worthington

Sebastopol, CA • 707.823.3581
www.domjoy.com

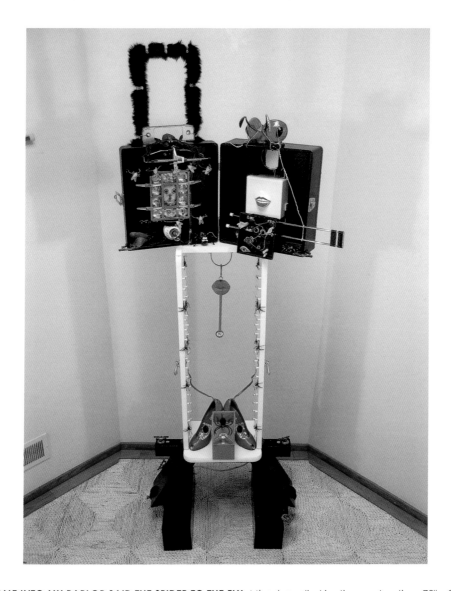

COME INTO MY PARLOR SAID THE SPIDER TO THE FLY. Mixed-media kinetic construction. 72" x 32"

"I place my images on a tightrope between comic absurdity and tragic consequence. This piece is based on the poem by Mary Howitt, *The Spider and the Fly*. In the artwork, I explore different manifestations of entrapment, flattery, and human behavior, encouraging viewer participation to enhance emotional interaction." Venues: Jan Baum Gallery, Judith Fein-Representative.

Jesse Holmes

Boulder, CO • 303.447.8823
www.jesseholmes.com

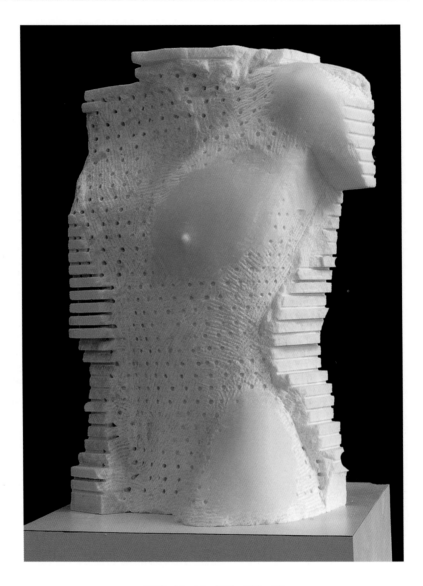

APRIL. Marble. 22" x 13" x 9"

"The figure looks its best in marble! No other material retains the sensuality and the planned foresight required by a sculptor to make a work of art that has so much tradition and cultural value that engages the human form."

Massimo Righini

Washington, DC • 202.265.0943
www.sculpture.org/massimorighini

HYPOCRITE I - THE TELEVANGELIST. Tiger's eye alabaster. 14' x 10' x 8'

"I have always had a profound distrust for those who tell us with great certainty that we are all miserable sinners and should reject the temptations of a material world under pain of eternal damnation. So when they fall to their natural instincts, shed crocodile tears, and beg for forgiveness, their misbehavior should be forgiven but not forgotten. He should not burn in hell, but brethren, pray tell. Would he be so distraught if he hadn't been caught?" Venue: L'Enfant Gallery.

Bethanie Brandon

San Rafael, CA • 415.492.0809
www.bethaniebrandondesign.com

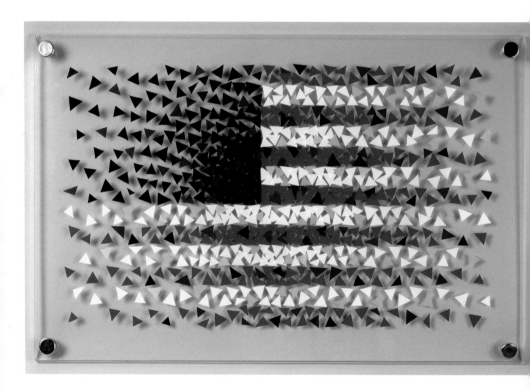

FRAGILE. Mixed media. 22" x 34" x 1"

"This piece is constructed using silk and nylon triangles adhered between two layers of plexiglass with steel corner bolts."

Myra Burg

Santa Monica, CA • 310.399.5040
www.myraburg.com

QUIET OBOES IN WINTER COLOR. Wrapped fiber. 2" to 5" d

"Essentially cylindrical tapestries, these *Quiet Oboes* become jewelry for the walls they adorn. The inspiration comes from having begun as a weaver and having become an architect. The *Oboes* are only a part of that delightful evolution." Venues: Earthenworks Gallery, Black's Orange Floral Shop, New Morning Gallery.

Suzanne Donazetti

Raton, NM • 505.445.8040
www.freefalldesigns.com

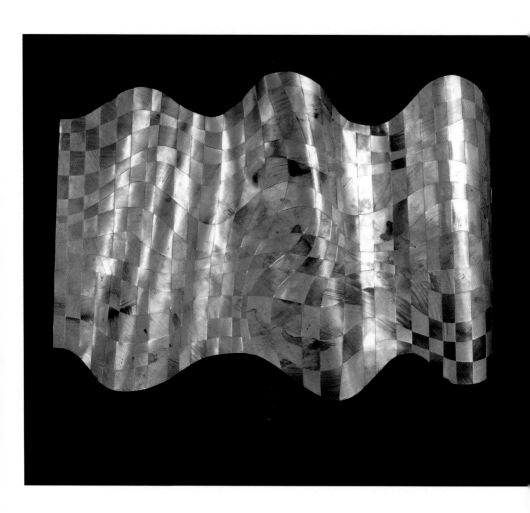

NEPENTHE. Acrylic on copper, woven. 14" x 20" x 4"

"Through color and the refractive lens of weaving, I try to communicate the harmony to be found in the natural environment. I paint two landscapes on gilded copper and weave them together to create abstract experiences for meditation and emotion." Venues: Crossroads Contemporary, Artist Showcase, A. Jain Marunouchi Gallery.

Morris D. Dorenfeld

Spruce Head, ME
207.594.5142

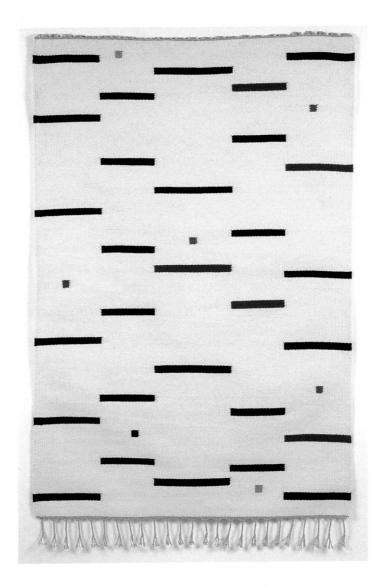

DOMINO IV. Tapestry. 66" x 46"

"Using little color, the *Domino* series weavings is a new direction for me. Relying on the dynamic, classic contrast of black and white, the composition is built with modest repetition. Less is more...I like that."

Wendy Ellertson

Boston, MA • 617.785.8750
www.ellertson.com

MRETRAC, THE ASSERTIVE. Painted leather, hand felting, wire, wood. 39" x 36" x 28"

"My work reflects the adage by Joseph Campbell that an important role of the artist is to mythologize the world and environment. I create unique, story-filled mythic figures combining leather, wood, fiber, and clay with an eclectic array of ancient and contemporary, techniques, and dreams." Venues: ACC Shows, Paradise City Arts Festivals, Ann Arbor Street Art Fair.

Sally Elliott

Boulder, CO • 303.443.6224
sdelliott@mindspring.com

SALLY'S SKIRT OF MANY COLORS. Gouache on paper. 40" x 30"

"This series of paintings uses clothing belonging to me or to family members. The skirt bursts into a frame of seaweed and Manta Ray egg cases, also known as 'witches pocketbooks,' fall into the skirt. My work is informed by dream imagery, objects of personal significance, Magic Realism, Asian perspective, saturated color, and abstract texture." Venues: Sandy Carson Gallery, Spark Cooperative Gallery.

PAGES TORN 3/1. Textile collage. 57" x 42"

"I began as a quilt-maker. In 1998, I began creating paper collages, collecting materials from all sources: books, maps, papers, paints, found objects. To blend the media of fiber and print, I began experimenting with a color copy machine. The collages were enlarged, copied onto heat transfer paper, and transferred onto fabric."

Jóh Ricci

New Oxford, PA • 717.624.5759
http://home.onemain.com/~earthwalk

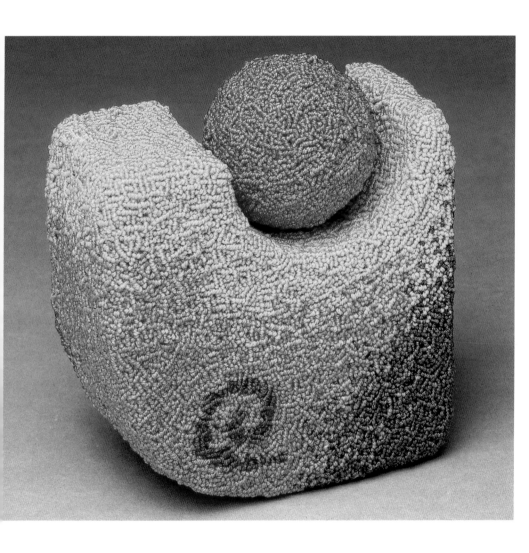

SUMMER SUN. Hand-dyed nylon cord. 4.75" x 4.25" x 2.25"

"It's 'knot' what you think! To create my one-of-a-kind contemporary baskets, my primary technique is knotting, although netting, crocheting, and hand-beadweaving may also be applied in combination with one another. My goal is to create expressive fiber forms that transcend the boundaries of the concept of the traditional basket." Venues: Snyderman-Works Galleries, Philadelphia Museum of Art Craft Show, Smithsonian Craft Show.

Flora Rosefsky

Atlanta, GA • 404.633.7896
www.florageart.com

SONGS OF PRAISE. Paper cutout, gouache, pastel, fabric collage. 40" x 60"

"My collage work, often described as joyful, interweaves the secular world with a unique spirituality. Whether narrative, symbolic, or purely from imagery that inspires me, I incorporate experiences of family and nature, creating images that are both universal and intimate."

Marion Philipsen Seasholtz

Johnson, VT • 802.635.2731
www.windsedgestudio.com

CITRUS WEAVE. Cotton batiks, silk. 102" x 92"

"I create quilts, pillows, and wall hangings using silk, velvet, cotton batiks, metallics, and brocades as well as some of my own nature-inspired, block-printed fabrics. I enjoy combining the different textures, colors, and contrast of these fabrics in variations of traditional patterns as well as my own original designs." Venues: Grovewood Gallery, ACC shows, Paradise City Arts.

Maria Simonsson

Alexandria, VA • 301.589.4640
mariasimonsson@mac.com

VIKING II. Fiber sculpture. 20" x 16"

"Three-dimensional shapes are fascinating to me and uncommon in the world of textiles.
I enjoy pushing the boundary of the expected. I start with a wire framework, usually a
recognizable vessel shape: basket, urn, or boat. I cover it with fabric which I stitch, like a three-
dimensional quilt. Finally, I add embellishments. Shape, texture, and pattern come together."

Cathy Smith

Frenchtown, NJ • 908.996.1233
www.cathysmithdesigns.com

PRINCESS TRINA. Cotton, silk, leather, found objects. 20" h

"I love color, mixing patterns, textures, and the human form, so I create figurative art dolls."
Venues: ACC Baltimore, Craftproducers Shows

Andrea Tucker-Hody

San Anselmo, CA • 415.456.4402
goldenleafpaper@aol.com

SNOW CRANE. Hand-made paper, gold leaf drawing, copper bars. 32" x 24"

"I describe my *washi* (hand-made paper assemblages) as *papestries*. Layered and textured, with pure Japanese aesthetics, the assemblages assimilate various cultural histories. Echoing my background in printmaking, I utilize gold leaf like an etching plate—drawing through it and glazing the surfaces. Pieces range in size from one to six feet and are made of hand-dyed fiber poured and laminated onto flexible screens, permitting the interplay of space, light, and fiber."

Lawrence Wheeler

Westford, MA • 978.392.0073
www.wheelerbaskets.com

THE CLEAR MONOFILAMENT JAR. Monofilament nylon, rattan, Corian. 7" x 5" x 5"

"The *Clear Monofilament Jar* was my attempt to make a basket that could be thought of as a 'ghost basket,' both there and not. Clear monofilament nylon creates the almost transparent effect woven over near-white rattan staves. I turned a pure white Corian top and base to complete the effect." Venues: ACC Baltimore and St. Paul, Crafts at the Castle Show.

Jane Woolverton

San Francisco, CA • 415.285.7443
janewoolverton@aol.com

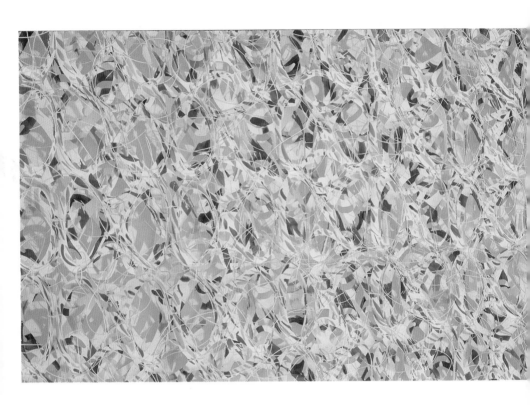

L'ETE. Plastic six-pack holders, acrylic, thread. 58" x 62"

"Working with plastic six-pack holders, I endeavor to create a transformation, allowing the material properties to evolve into a different understanding. The recycled holders, when assembled and hung together, become large fiber sculptures, consisting of two, three, or more layers." Venues: Pacific Rim Sculptors, Sanchez Art Center, San Francisco Open Studio.

Dianne Zimbabwe

Roxbury, MA • 617.445.0799
www.diannezimbabwe.com

OWNER OF STORIES. Mudcloth. 36" x 33"

"*Owner of Stories*, a contemporary *bogolanfini*, or mudcloth, was born from the marriage of a majestic little neighbor living in my backyard in Roxbury, Massachusetts with the name given by the Ashanti people of West Africa to their famous trickster, Kwaku Ananse." Venues: National Heritage Museum, First Night Boston, Pen and Brush Gallery.

Constance Bergfors

Cabin John, MD • 301.229.3503
bergfors@comcast.net

THE POLITICIANS. English walnut. 109" x 100" x 24"

"My wood sculpture is like poetry in space. I think about rhythms, space, light, and movement. I want the work to appear ready to move. Touch is also part of the poetry. I could still make sculpture even if I became blind. I could feel the movement and the space."

Dave Boykin

Denver, CO • 303.294.0703
www.boykinpearce.com

BUREAU WITH MIRROR. Mahogany, pommele sapele. 15" x 71" x 20"

"In this ensemble, we seek elegance through strong but subtle form-oriented design and deliberate material selection."

RECUERDO/MEMORY. Aspen. 33" x 11" x 11"

"This piece began with fallen aspen branches gathered in the mountains. The wood was simply carved and lightly painted retaining its organic qualities. Combined with the carved wood are man-made artifacts. I use materials as visual metaphors alluding to the delicate symbiosis between human culture and the natural world." Venues: Philadelphia Buyers Market of American Craft, Left Bank Gallery, Obsidian Gallery.

Robert Hargrave

Tallahassee, FL • 850.224.5289
www.plywoodsculpture.com

MOST FAVORED VESSEL & ARCH TABLE. Wood. 36" x 8" x 12" and 36" x 14" x 30"

"*Most Favored Vessel* is laminated and carved plywoods and *Arch Table* is laminated and carved walnut and maple. They are two different designs related only by shape and style."

Jan Jacque

Livonia, NY • 585.346.6772
www.janjacque.com

TRUE HEART. Tiger maplewood, ceramic. 18" x 10" x 3"

"First, the delicate balance and beautiful complexity of nature excite my imagination and touch my design. Then, with tactile materials (clay and wood), I 'inspirit' my vessels and mirrors with an essence of earth, growth, water, and our connection to life."

Bill Luce

Renton, WA • 425.277.6461
www.billluce.com

STRATA SERIES. Round-bottomed vessel. Douglas fir. 4.5" x 6"

"My inspiration for this series comes from layers found in nature such as those in sedimentary rock. For the past few years, I've focused on pushing the limits of difficult and traditionally unturnable woods while continuing my study of the influence a material's visible elements have on the emotional impact of a vessel's form." Venues: Patina Gallery, del Mano Gallery, American Art Company Gallery.

Alice Porembski

Redding, CA • 530.243.6132
treesknees@sbcglobal.net

TABLE. Private commission. Walnut, lacewood, ebony. 24" x 18" x 96"

"As an aesthetic response to bring focus and importance to a client's collection of objects, this table presents a dialogue between grain patterns in California walnut and Australian lacewood. Ebony details the base, which interlocks with the top and shelf."

John A. Schaffner

St. Leonard, MD • 410.586.1652
johnaschaffner@comcast.net

NEMATODA. Wood. 8" x 8" x 180"

"When creating my sculptures, I use natural materials, thus creating an object based on organic shapes in nature. The various textures, shapes, and the negative space hide nothing but bring out an exceptional quality of this old but contemporary material. Producing a piece of sculpture is similar to having a puzzle and solving it aesthetically." Venues: Torpedo Factory Art Center, Designers Two, CalvART Gallery.

LE DUET. Mahogany, English walnut. 26" x 20"

"Part of my role as an artist is to remind myself—and the viewer—to smile. For twenty-five years I have created unique pieces of sculpture, furniture, and entrance doors, affirming the sensuous and playful nature of wood. The play of Cubism in this piece allows us to enjoy an already appreciated form in a new way. If you listen, you can hear their sweet song."

Jacques Vesery

Damariscotta, ME • 207.563.8965
jvesery@tidewater.net

THE FLOW OF SKY TO SEA. Carved and textured cherry, dyed silver leaf, blue florite. 4" x 2.5"

"Exploring texture exposes our minds to the wonders of hidden beauty around us in every part of life. An engaging convergence of color, texture, and proportion in any object forms a unique spirit and soul from birth...material and technique then become irrelevant. *C'est tres important pour moi.*"
Venues: del Mano Gallery, Elan Fine Arts, Midtown Payson Galleries.

Artist Index

Part One: 2D

Part Two: 3D

Ceramics

Glass

Jewelry

Metal

Mixed Media

Stone

Textiles & Fiber

Wood

Photo Credits

VENUES

44T Artspace
Denver, CO   303.433.1073

A. Jain Marunouchi
New York, NY   212.969.9660

Abend Gallery Fine Art
Denver, CO   303.355.0950

ADA Gallery
Richmond, VA   804.644.0100

Alarion Gallery
Boulder, CO   800.523.9177

Alex Gallery
Washington, DC   202.667.2599

Alliance of Women Artists
Greenbrae, CA   415.461.9054

Altitude Art Gallery
Bozeman, MT   406.582.4472

American Craft Council (ACC) Shows
Baltimore, MD   February
Atlanta, GA   March
St. Paul, MN   April
San Francisco, CA   August
Charlotte, NC   November
Sarasota, FL   December

American Craft Expo
Evanston, IL   August

American Painting
Washington, DC   202.244.3244

Anderson O'Brien Fine Art
Omaha, NE   402.390.0717

Andrea Schwartz Gallery
San Francisco, CA   415.495.2090

Arches Gallery
Healdsburg, CA   707.431.1396

Art + Artisans Consulting
Houston, TX   713.874.0051

Art Design Consultants
Cincinnati, OH   513.723.1222

Art on 5th Gallery
Austin, TX   512.481.1111

Art Resources Gallery
Edina, MN   952.922.1770

ArtCenter Manatee
Bradenton, FL   941.746.2862

Arte Misia Gallery
Sedona, AZ   928.282.3686

Artisans Gallery
San Rafael, CA   415.460.5208

Artists Guild of San Francisco
San Francisco, CA   415.835.0610

Artizen Fine Arts
Dallas, TX   214.979.2140

ArtReach
Albuqerque, NM   505.822.8900

ArtSeen, Inc.
Bethesda, MD   301.229.2665

ARTworkSF
San Francisco, CA   415.673.3080

Aspen Art Museum
Aspen, CO   970.925.8050

Asylum Gallery
Sacramento, CA   916.804.6095

Aurora Colors Gallery
Petaluma, CA   707.762.0131

Austin Presence
Austin, TX   512.306.9636

Berkeley Potters Guild Sale
Berkeley, CA   Dec., May

Beverly McNeil Gallery
Destin, FL   850.654.4322

Bill Lowe Gallery
Atlanta, GA   404.352.8114

Blue Horse Fine Art
Lyons, CO   303.823.5839

Bluewood Gallery
Brevard, NC   828.883.4142

Boca Raton Museum of Art
Boca Raton, FL   561.392.2500

Boulder Open Studios
Boulder, CO   303.444.1862

Bowman Gallery
New York, NY   917.860.9869

Breckenridge Fine Art Gallery
Breckenridge, CO   970.453.9500

Broadway Gallery
Fairfax, Virginia   703.273.2388

Buchanan Gallery
Galveston, TX   409.763.8683

California Modern Gallery
San Francisco, CA   415.503.0944

CalvART Gallery
Prnc. Frdrk, MD   410.535.9252

Camera Obscura Gallery
Denver, CO   303.623.4059

Carlson Fine Arts
Sausalito, CA   415.331.9520

Carolina Designer Craftsmen
Raleigh, NC   November

Casa Galleria
San Jn. Btista., CA   831.623.4635

Chemers Gallery
Tustin, CA   714.731.5432

Chesapeake Gallery
Prnc. Frdrk., MD   410.257.1420

Chiaroscuro Gallery
Scottsdale, AZ   480.429.0711

Christensen Heller Gallery
5831 College Avenue
Oakland, CA   510.655.5952
www.chistensenheller.com

Fine art and crafts—focusing on ancient to modern jewelry, and on recycled materials

Coady Contemporary
Santa Fe, NM   505.988.1175

Coleman Gallery Contemp. Art
Albuquerque NM   505.232.0224

Columbus Jewelry Show
Columbus, OH   614.221.2237

Cramer Gallery
Vnyd. Haven, MA   508.696.7323

Creation Art Gallery
Juno Beach, FL   561.296.3566

Crossroads Contemporary
Santa Fe, NM   505.982.5700

Dayle Dunn Gallery
Hf. Moon Bay, CA 650.726.7667

del Mano Gallery
Los Angeles, CA   800.335.6266

Denise Roberge' Gallery
Palm Desert, CA   760.340.5045

Elan Fine Arts
Rockport, ME   207.236.4401

Elder Gallery
Charlotte, NC   704.370.6337

Eleonore Austerer Gallery
Palm Desert, CA   760.346.3695

Erdreich White Fine Art
Boston, MA   617.266.0644

Evolving Art Gallery
San Francisco, CA 415.255.9091

Exhibitrek, The Gallery
Boulder, CO   303.998.1711

Exploding Head Gallery
Sacramento, CA   916.442.8424

Fire Opal Gallery
Jmca. Plain, MA   617.524.0262

Flanders Art Gallery
Raleigh, NC   919.834.5044

Fore Street Gallery
Portland, ME   207.874.8084

Frank J. Miele Gallery
New York, NY   212.249.7250

Freed Gallery
Lincoln City, OR   541.994.5600

g2 Gallery
Scottsdale, AZ   480.429.7729

Gallery 22
Cincinnati, OH   513.489.2568

Gallery on Main
Richmond, KY   859.527.3334

Gasparilla Festival of the Arts
Tampa, FL   813.876.1747

George Krevsky Gallery
San Francisco, CA 415.397.9748

Glass Garage Gallery West
Hollywood, CA   310.639.5228

Great Indoors
Broomfield, CO   720.566.1053

Highlight Gallery
Mendocino, CA   707.937.3132

I. Wolk Gallery
St. Helena, CA   707.963.8800

Idyllwild Gallery
Idyllwild, CA   951.659.1948

Image City Photography Gallery
Rochester, NY   585.271.2540

Images Gallery
Boca Raton, FL   561.393.9115

Industrial Ctr. Bldg. Xmas Show
Sausalito, CA   December

Infusion Gallery
Los Angeles, CA   213.683.8827

iota Gallery
Dallas, TX   214.522.2999

J. Pierce White Oak Gallery
Minneapolis, MN   612.922.3575

Jan Baum Gallery
Los Angeles, CA   323.932.0170

Jessica Fine Art
Provincetown, MA 508.487.0884

Joan Resnikoff Gallery
Roxbury, MA   617.541.5380

Joe Wilcox Fine Arts
Sedona, AZ   800.282.2584

Jones & Terwilliger Galleries
Carmel, CA   888.278.0040

Joyce Gordon Gallery
Oakland, CA   510.465.8928

Judith Fein Artist Representative
Sebastopol, CA   707.829.7233

Kaviar Forge Gallery
Louisville, KY   502.561.0377

Kitrell/Riffkind
Dallas, TX   972.239.7957

Klay Gallery
Nyack, NY   845.348.6306

Lagerquist Gallery
Atlanta, GA   404.261.8273

Langman Gallery
Willow Grove, PA   215.657.8333

Lauryn Taylor Fine Art
Carmel, CA   831.624.1161

Left Bank Gallery
Wellfleet, MA   508.349.7939

L'Enfant Gallery
Washington, DC   202.625.2873

Loveland Sculpture Invitational
Loveland, CO   970.663.7467

Lucas Valley Open Studios
San Rafael, CA   November

Lumina Contemporary Art
Taos, NM   505.776.0123

Lydon Fine Art
Chicago, IL   312.943.1133

Lyons Head Gallery
Carmel, CA   831.659.4192

Main St. Gallery
Annapolis, MD   410.280.2787

Marin Art Festival
San Rafael, CA   June

Marin Open Studios
Marin County, CA May

Marin Society of Artists
Ross, CA   415.454.9561

Mariposa Gallery
Albuquerque, NM 505.268.6828

Mark Palmer Gallery
Paducah, KY   270.444.2056

Matt Jones Gallery
Tuscaloosa, AL   250.758.1228

Maxwell Fine Arts	**Q Gallery**	**Stone Griffin Gallery**
Peekskill, NY 914.737.8622	Orlando, FL 407.701.9382	Campbell, CA 408.374.2944
McLean Gallery	**Quicksilver Mine Company**	**Sue Greenwood Fine Art**
Malibu, CA 310.456.2226	Forestville, CA 707.887.0799	Laguna Bch., CA 949.494.0669
Meyerhoefer Gallery	**Raiford Gallery**	**Summit One Gallery**
Lake Worth, FL 561.533.5332	Roswell, GA 707.645.2050	Highlands, NC 828.526.2673
Micaëla Gallery	**Red Brick Gallery**	**Terra Gallery**
San Francisco, CA 415.551.8118	Aspen, CO 970.429.2777	Columbus, OH 614.228.4188
Michael B. Tusing Gallery	**Rice Gallery**	**The Gallery**
Staunton, VA 540.885.2697	Overland Park, KS 913.685.8889	Beaufort, SC 843.470.9994
Midtown Payson Galleries	**RiverView Gallery**	**Tower Gallery**
Hobe Sound, FL 772.546.2999	Havre de Grc., MD 410.939.6401	Sanibel, FL 239.472.4557
Midwest Jewelry Expo	**Robischon Gallery**	**Valley Art Gallery**
Madison WI 877.778.3537	Denver, CO 303.298.7788	Walnut Creek, CA 925.935.4311
Morgan Glass Gallery	**Rosenberg Kaufman Fine Art**	**Topaz Gallery**
Pittsburgh, PA 412.441.5200	New York, NY 212.431.4838	Atlanta, GA 404.995.0155
Museum of Contemporary Craft	**San Francisco Women Artists**	**Torpedo Factory Art Center**
Portland, OR 503.223.2656	San Francisco, CA 415.440.7392	Alexandria, VA 703.683.3535
Museum of Craft and Folk Art	**Sandra Phillips Gallery**	**Touchstone Gallery**
San Francisco, CA 415.227.4888	Denver, CO 303.573.5969	Washington, DC 202.347.2787
Neptune Gallery	**Sausalito Art Festival**	**Vetro Art Glass**
Bethesda, MD 301.718.0809	Sausalito, CA Labor Day	Grapevine, TX 817.251.1668
Nielsen Gallery	**Sculpture at Chesterwood**	**Vision Gallery**
Boston, MA 617.266.4835	Stockbridge, MA 413.298.3579	Chandler, AZ 480.917.6859
North Bay Art Works	**Sculpture New Hope**	**Ward Nasse Gallery**
Novato, CA 415.892.8188	New Hope, PA April – June	New York, NY 212.925.6951
Oxford Fine Arts Fair	**Select Art**	**Water Street Gallery**
Oxford, MD 410.226.5904	Dallas, TX 214.521.6833	Douglas, MI 269.857.8485
Palo Alto Clay & Glass Festival	**SFMOMA Artists Gallery**	**Weatherburn Gallery**
Palo Alto, CA July	San Francisco, CA 415.441.4777	Naples, FL 239.263.8056
Pamela Skinner Gallery	**Shidoni Galleries**	**William Torphy Fine Arts**
Sacramento, CA 916.446.1786	Tesuque, NM 505.988.8001	El Sobrante, CA 510.222.8215
Philadelphia Buyers Market	**Silver Fox Gallery**	**Winfield Gallery**
Philadelphia, PA 410.889.2933	Hendersonville, NC 828.698.0601	Carmel, CA 800.289.1950
Phoenix Gallery	**Snyderman/Works Gallery**	**Winterowd Fine Art**
Topeka, KS 785.272.3999	Philadelphia, PA 215.922.7775	Santa Fe, NM 505.992.8878
Potomac Craftsmen Fiber Gllry.	**Soho Myriad**	**Zenith Galley**
Alexandria, VA 703.548.0935	Atlanta, GA 404.351.5656	Washington, DC 202.783.2963
Prince Royal Gallery	**Soren Christensen Gallery**	**Zip 37 Gallery**
Alexandria, VA 703.548.5151	New Orleans, LA 504.569.9501	Denver, CO 303.477.4525